THE YOKE OF BONDAGE

THE YOKE OF BONDAGE

JIMMY SWAGGART MINISTRIES
P.O. Box 262550 | Baton Rouge, Louisiana 70826-2550
www.jsm.org

ISBN 978-1-941403-43-3

09-155 | COPYRIGHT © 2018 Jimmy Swaggart Ministries®

18 19 20 21 22 23 24 25 26 27 / TS / 10 9 8 7 6 5 4 3 2 1

TABLE OF CONTENTS

THE YOKE OF BONDAGE

INTRODUCTION

INTRODUCTION

AS IT REGARDS THE FREEDOM we have in Christ, I think the Holy Spirit used the apostle Paul as He used no other man. One might say that Jesus Christ is the new covenant, meaning that He does not merely have the new covenant or that he understands it more than anyone else, but, in fact, He is the new covenant. The meaning of the new covenant is the Cross. That meaning was given to the apostle Paul, and he gave it to us in his 14 epistles. Thereby, if one doesn't understand the Cross for salvation and sanctification, one does not understand the new covenant.

THE YOKE OF BONDAGE

Unless one knows Paul's teaching, simply put, one will not know how to live a life that is free of bondage and, in a sense, slavery. I realize that sounds strange as it regards Christians, but the sad truth is, while most Christians have an understanding of the Cross of Christ as it regards salvation, they have almost no understanding at all as it regards sanctification. I speak of how we live for God on a daily basis, how we grow in grace and the knowledge of the Lord, and how we have victory over the world, the flesh, and the Devil.

In this book I hope to address all of these subjects. If I am able to at least give a glimpse of that which the Lord gave to the apostle Paul, then my efforts will not have been wasted, and your time, as well, will have been well spent.

There is absolutely nothing more important than this subject that we will attempt to address. It is the will of God that we walk in victory. While the Bible does not teach sinless perfection, it most definitely does teach that sin is not to have dominion over us (Rom. 6:14). In a sense, bondage and dominion are basically the same. To be sure, that's a miserable existence for a child of God, and yet, virtually the entirety of the modern church is living in a state of bondage, i.e., the yoke of bondage.

THE CROSS

In 1997, the Lord spoke to my heart and gave me the solution to this very problem of bondage. He said:

"The answer for which you seek is found in the Cross.

"The solution for which you seek is found in the Cross.

"The answer for which you seek is found *only* in the Cross."

A little later, He explained to me how the Cross was and is the answer. He showed me that the Cross of Christ is the means by which everything is given to us by the Lord. In other words, when Jesus atoned for all sin—past, present, and future—in the giving of Himself as the perfect sacrifice on the Cross, this opened the door for everything that we receive from God. The old covenant could not do such. It could only point to that which was to come, which was the new covenant, and, in essence, which was the Cross.

——◇——

Arm of the Lord! awake, awake!
Put on Thy strength, the nations shake;
And let the world adoring, see
Triumphs of mercy wrought by Thee.

Say to the heathen, from Thy throne,
I am Jehovah, God alone.
Thy voice their idols shall confound,
And cast their altars to the ground.

Let Zion's time of favor come;
Oh, bring the tribes of Israel home:
And let our wondering eyes behold
Gentiles and Jews in Jesus' fold.

Almighty God, Thy grace proclaim
In every clime, of every name;
Let adverse powers before Thee fall,
And crown the Saviour Lord of all.

THE YOKE OF BONDAGE

CHAPTER 1

LIBERTY

LIBERTY

"STAND FAST THEREFORE IN the liberty wherewith Christ has made us free, and be not entangled again with the yoke of bondage" (Gal. 5:1).

THE KEY VERSE

There are two particulars that Paul engaged:
1. He defended his apostleship, which included a defense of his right to preach the gospel with or without the support of other human authorities (Gal. 1:11-2:21).
2. He defended the gospel itself, showing that it is by grace alone and entirely apart from human works that the Christian is set free from the curse of the law and brought into a right relationship with God (Gal. 3:1-4:31).

However, there is another point that the apostle here makes. That is that the liberty into which believers are called is not a liberty that leads to license, as his opponents—of which there seemed to be many—charged. It was rather a liberty that leads to a mature responsibility and holiness before God through the power of the indwelling Holy Spirit. This theme dominates much of Paul's writings.

I personally believe that Galatians 5:1 is a key verse to all that he believed and taught.

Because of the nature of the true gospel and of the work of Christ on his behalf, the believer is now to turn away from anything that smacks of legalism. He is, instead, to rest in Christ's triumphant work for him and live in the power of the Holy Spirit. It probably can be said that this verse could be divided into two parts:

1. It is a declaration of Christ's purpose in saving us. We might say that it is for freedom that Christ has set us free.
2. Also, we must stand firm and not let ourselves be burdened again by a yoke of slavery.

THE YOKE OF THE LAW

Since the Jews of Paul's time spoke of taking the yoke of the law upon oneself, it is likely that Paul is referring to such an expression here. To the Jews, the taking of the law's yoke was good; indeed, it was the essence of religion.

To Paul, it was assuming the yoke of slavery. Perhaps Paul was also remembering that Jesus had spoken of Christians taking His yoke upon them (Mat. 11:29-30), but this involves a different kind of service—one that is easy and light—as the believer quickly begins to see, that is, if he looks at this thing correctly.

Considering the stand that Paul took, and thank God that he did, it is certain that the Judaizers came to hate him severely. He minced no words when he spoke, pulled no punches, cleared the ground of all clutter, and left no room for their doctrine. In other words, he took no prisoners.

THE LIBERTY MADE POSSIBLE BY CHRIST

The phrase, *"Stand fast therefore in the liberty wherewith Christ has made us free,"* centers up in the word *liberty*.

The teaching is that Christ died on the Cross to give us the advantage of having this liberty (freedom). This liberty consists of the Christian's freedom from the law and, thereby, freedom to live a holy life.

Under the law, a person has no more liberty than a child under a guardian. A child has no freedom of action or right of self-determination. He must move within a set of rules described by his guardian. He is not old enough to act alone. He must always act under the restrictions of his guardian. So it is with the person under law, and we might say law of any kind.

Here were these Galatian Christians, free from the law, having been placed in the family of God as adult sons. They were indwelt by the Holy Spirit, who would enable them to act out in their experience their maturity of Christian life in which they were placed. However, now they were putting on the straightjacket of the law, cramping their experience, stultifying their actions, and depriving themselves of the power of the Holy Spirit. In other words, they were going from freedom to bondage.

They were like adults putting themselves under rules made for children.

LIBERTY AS TO THE METHOD

The liberty spoken of here does not refer to the kind of life a person lives, and neither does it have reference to his words and actions. Instead, it has to do with the method by which one lives one's life.

The Judaizers lived their lives by dependence on self-effort in an attempt to obey the law. In other words, these were individuals who claimed to have accepted Christ, but at the same time, insisted that all who followed Christ must also keep the law, and we speak of the law of Moses. Paul, in essence, told them and all concerned that this was the sure road to disaster; hence, one going in that direction was putting himself into a yoke of bondage.

In fact, the Judaizers lived their lives by dependence on self-effort in an attempt to obey the law. By contrast, the Galatian Christians had been living their lives with dependence upon the indwelling Holy Spirit, which is God's way.

Their hearts had been occupied with the Lord Jesus, with the details of their lives being guided by the ethics that emerged from the teaching of the apostles, both doctrinal and practical.

Now, in swinging over to law, they were losing that freedom of action and that flexibility of self-determination that one exercises in the doing of what is right when one does right. I'm speaking of doing right, not because the law forbids the wrong and commands the right, but because it is right, because it pleases the Lord Jesus, and because of love for Him. Paul exhorts them to keep on standing fast in that freedom from law.

To be factual, with the Holy Spirit leading and guiding the believer, He demands far more of us than law ever did. But yet, whatever it is that He demands, He gives us the power to do what needs to be done. Then, we find that there is no problem or trouble in the doing of it, whatever it might be.

BASIC DIRECTION

Paul shows in the first chapter of the book of Galatians that he was divinely commissioned as an apostle—and by the Lord Jesus at that—and as such was not answerable to the Twelve in Jerusalem, etc.

In his epistle to the Galatians, he defends his doctrine of justification by faith alone against the Judaizers, who added works to faith as the necessary conditions for salvation.

We will find in Chapter 5 of Galatians that the inspired apostle will present practical teaching and exhortation that was designed to correct the habit that the teaching of the Judaizers was causing in the personal lives of the Galatian Christians, and anyone else for that matter with whom they came in contact. In Galatians 4:19, Paul expresses the wish that the Lord Jesus might again be outwardly expressed in their lives.

The Galatians had lost the beauty of Christ, which, before the coming of the Judaizers, had been so prominent in their experience. The Lord Jesus was not being expressed in their lives as heretofore. This was the direct result of the Judaizers' legalistic teachings.

Wuest said, "The Galatian Christians, instead of depending on the indwelling Spirit to produce in their lives the beauty of the Lord Jesus, now were depending upon self-effort in an attempt to obey the law of Moses. Accordingly, Paul's practical teaching emphasizes the ministry of the Holy Spirit, and the Galatians are exhorted to put themselves again under His control."

WHAT DOES PAUL MEAN BY LIBERTY?

He is actually speaking of liberty from the yoke of the law, and, of course, we're speaking here of the law of Moses, but it could pertain to any law. If one wants to know what the law of Moses actually is, and I speak of all law, he should look at the last half of the book of Exodus and the book of Leviticus. As any Christian knows, at least those who study their Bibles, it was a very involved process. Actually, the law of Moses was given by God for specific purposes. It was never intended to save anyone for the simple reason that it had no saving grace. The following are some of the reasons for the law:

- It was given by God to show His standard of righteousness, in other words, what He expected of man.
- It was given to define sin, in other words, what exactly sin was.
- It was given to show man how inadequate that he was, and, in fact, to show that, due to the fall, he could not keep these simple laws, as simple as they were.

- Actually, this law, oftentimes referred to as the law of Moses, was the fairest law on the face of the earth. It treated all alike and played no favorites.

One might say that the law was given that man may know what God expected, what, as stated, was God's standard of righteousness, and, as well, what was God's perfect standard of morality.

The law was given not only to show man how bad he actually was but, as well, to show him how good he wasn't.

Instead of taking the law and applying it to their lives as the Lord intended, Israel perverted it by attempting to make salvation out of its precepts. How did they do this?

ISRAEL'S ERRONEOUS INTERPRETATION

They twisted the law and failed to see it as God gave it, and they did so by their own efforts and works. In other words, they set up their own system of rules as to how to keep the law instead of actually asking God for His help. By the time of Christ, they had actually added over 600 oral laws to the original law. These laws were referred to as fence laws, with many even claiming that the oral, man-devised laws were more important even than those given by God.

As we have previously stated, trying to keep the law by one's own ability or to bring about some desired result always brings about the very opposite result: pride and self-righteousness. However, with deception being the name of the game, most do not see that within themselves.

By the time of Christ, the burden upon the people had become very grievous, with the whole country of Israel having become a hotbed of legalism. In fact, Rome stated that of all the Roman Empire, the tiny state of Israel, or Judaea as it was then called, was the most difficult to control. Roman historians proclaimed the Jews of that day as the meanest people on the face of the earth, hating all of mankind. To be sure, they were not far wrong, if wrong at all!

THE LAW ACTUALLY POINTED TO JESUS

In fact, every single thing in the law of Moses pointed to Christ. All of the sacrifices in which Israel engaged constantly were but types and portrayals of Christ, especially as it regarded His vicarious, atoning work that He would carry out on the Cross. The feast days, as well, all pointed to His ministry in some capacity. Everything pointed to Him. In fact, Jesus was the true Israel, the true law, the true church, and the true man. So, it seems that they would have recognized Him when He ultimately came, but they didn't! The reason was because of the manner in which they now approached the law. They were perverting it, trying to keep it in all the wrong ways—by their strength and ability and apart from God.

The Lord certainly wanted them to keep the law, even commanded that they keep the law, which should be obvious. Still, it was the manner and way in which they attempted to keep the law that was so reprehensible to God. This ultimately caused their destruction.

It is the same today in living for the Lord. The question should be asked, *how* are we living for the Lord? By that, I mean: Are we attempting to do so in our own strength, or are we allowing Christ to live in us, which He does by the power, person, and agency of the Holy Spirit? So, when we look at it in that fashion, we realize that many in the church are having the same problem that Israel of old had. There was no way that anyone in Israel could keep the law in his own strength, and neither can a believer live for Christ in that manner. Israel's only hope then was faith in the promises of God, and it is our only hope presently. In fact, it always has been that way (Gen. 15:6).

THE CROSS AND THE LAW

Every believer in the world is either under the Cross (grace) or under law. If the believer doesn't understand the Cross of Christ relative to our sanctification, that believer is under law, which makes for a miserable existence.

Most Christians have at least a working knowledge of the Cross of Christ as it refers to salvation, but none at all as it refers to sanctification. That is strange considering that almost all of Paul's writings concerned the Cross of Christ—the great sacrifice of Christ—as it refers to our sanctification. In other words, we are speaking of how we live for God on a daily basis, how we have victory over the world, the flesh, and the Devil, and how we grow in grace and the knowledge of the Lord.

Let me say it again: If we are not functioning under grace, which can only be done by our faith being placed totally and completely in Christ and what Christ did for us at the Cross, we are automatically under law, whether we realize it or not.

Of course, when we speak of law at the present, we are mostly speaking of law that is devised by ourselves, our church, preachers, religious denominations, etc. Irrespective, if it's not Christ and the Cross, whether we realize it or not, it is law, and under law, we have all kinds of problems. That's the reason for the difficulties of most Christians.

BONDAGE

Any system of lawkeeping will always create bondage, for that is what it is designed to do. It imprisons one as one struggles and fights to try to obey its precepts, which, all the time, man is unable to do, at least in his own strength. In effect, he becomes a slave, and it will happen under modern law (laws of our design to help us draw closer to God, etc.) just as quickly as it happened under the ancient Mosaic law.

It would seem that any Christian ought to know that, but to be sure, only a few do. Those who now know and understand the Cross relative to sanctification, and their place in that sacrifice offered, will most surely understand that of which I speak. They know the freedom it brings. When they compare the two—salvation by lawkeeping (which actually does not exist) and salvation by grace (which comes through the Cross, and only through the Cross)—the difference is astounding. It is the difference of slavery and sonship, the difference of failure and victory, and the difference of sin and salvation. It is just that simple!

WHEN JESUS COMES INTO THE HEART

Upon the acceptance of Christ, all of this ends (I speak of lawkeeping), or at least it is supposed to end, with the Christian now experiencing freedom in Christ.

How does that work?

As we've just said, Christ was the true law. By that, I mean that He was the original giver of the law, and, as well, He is the only keeper of the law; however, the keeping of the law was as the true man. He kept the law perfectly, never failing one single time, and He did so on our behalf.

While that took care of our life and living, we now have the broken law to be addressed. He did that by going to the Cross and suffering its penalty, which He did voluntarily. Jesus Christ was not executed. Rome and Israel may have thought that was what was happening, but, in truth, He was not executed at all. He rather gave His life, offering it up freely as an atoning sacrifice. So, we must say that His death was not an assassination and not an execution, but rather a sacrifice.

When He rose from the dead and, thereby, walked out of that tomb, not a single sin or curse of the law followed Him. He had settled every account, had paid every debt, had cleansed every sin, and had defeated every demon, every fallen angel, and Satan himself. Consequently, for those who accept Him as their Lord and Saviour, they are free from all of those past things, with all of it having been done away in Christ. As the true man on my behalf and your behalf, He satisfied every legal debt that was owed by man to God and thereby broke the grip of sin. He defeated totally and completely every power of darkness.

OUR REPRESENTATIVE MAN

As we have stated and will continue to state, He did this all as our representative man, and He did it all for us. Surely one would know and realize that inasmuch as He did so much and at such price, He certainly wants us to have the benefits of all of these things He has done. Consequently, the moment we pick up one single law and attempt to find grace or victory in one iota of self-effort, we have negated the work of the Cross. Even though the things we may be doing are very scriptural and proper, and even necessary in their own way, nothing must be used in any manner that turns them into a law. I speak of such things as prayer, fasting, etc. Such insults Christ to the highest heaven and in effect says that the great price He paid was insufficient, and we must add our efforts to what He has already done in order to make it complete.

Such angers God because it insults Him. At the same time, the Lord knows that such direction will lead only to destruction.

One's faith must be totally in Christ and what He did at Calvary. One must appropriate that to oneself on a daily basis (Lk. 9:23) and trust totally in the Cross for victory in all things. It is faith, faith, faith! However, it must be faith in the right thing. By that, I mean that the Cross of Christ must ever be the object of our faith.

ENTER THE HOLY SPIRIT

The Holy Spirit will work only within the legal confines of Calvary (Rom. 8:1-3). Faith in the Cross automatically guarantees the help of the Holy Spirit with victory assured and guaranteed; however, the Holy Spirit will not help you to keep the law, and I mean a law of any nature. I think I can say without any fear of contradiction that He will not even help you to keep the Ten Commandments. He will not do such simply because Jesus as the true man has already kept all of the commandments. He has kept them perfectly, and He did so all on our behalf. When we properly understand our place and position in Christ, even as it refers to the Cross, the commandments are automatically kept, and now they are kept properly and in the way that God meant for them to be kept. As well, that's the only way they can be kept, which is what Paul's teaching is all about, and which the entirety of this scenario is all about.

The Holy Spirit lives within all believers. His help is available at all times, but it is help that will be given only on His terms. Those terms are the terms of the Cross and the sacrifice offered there.

WILL A PROPER UNDERSTANDING OF THE CROSS STOP ALL TEMPTATION?

No! As we have said over and over again: it's all a matter of faith, and I speak of faith in the Cross, in other words, what Jesus there did. However, Satan is going to try one's faith, and that trial will come in two ways:

1. Does the believer actually have faith in Christ and the Cross, or is he merely paying lip service to such or giving it mental affirmation only? Those things are not fake, and the probing of the Evil One, which the Lord allows, will soon prove whether our faith is real or not. Peter said, *"Who are kept by the power of God through faith unto salvation ready to be revealed in the last time. Wherein you greatly rejoice, though now for a season, if need be, you are in heaviness through mani-fold temptations: That the trial of your faith, being much more precious than of gold that perishes, though it be tried with fire, might be found unto praise and honor and glory at the appear-ing of Jesus Christ"* (I Pet. 1:5-7).

He also said, *"Beloved, think it not strange concerning the fiery trial which is to try you, as though some strange thing happened unto you"* (I Pet. 4:12). If one is to notice, Peter said, in effect, that this trying of our faith is going to continue until the appearing of Jesus Christ. So, Satan will not stop.

In fact, even after they have firmly anchored their faith in the Cross and are sure of what they believe, many believers will at times still be tripped up by the Devil and will sin. At that time, the Evil One will make charges thick and fast that the Cross is like all of these other things—it will not work either. However, the believer is to ask the Lord for for-giveness, get back up, and start once again on this road of faith in Christ. In fact, this may be repeated any number of times. All of this is a part of the trial of our faith, and this I guarantee: If you will not quit and will keep believing, then total, absolute, and complete victory will ultimately be yours. While God certainly never gets any glory out of sin, He definitely does get glory out of victory over sin, and that is what the Holy Spirit is all about.

2. The believer must evidence this faith even on a daily basis. In other words, this is not a onetime thing that will suffice from here to eternity. The faith I had in the Cross for yesterday won't do for today. That's the reason Jesus told us to take up the Cross daily (Lk. 9:23). The person is to keep believing. He must continue to believe and continue to make it known—to himself, to others, to God, and even to the Devil—that his faith is not in himself, not in his own ability, and not in his talents, education, or motivation. His faith must be totally and completely in Christ, and more particularly, it must be in what He did at Calvary.

At least one of the reasons that the Lord has designed this faith walk in this fashion is because of the propensity of man to fall into pride, which even the best of us can do. A constant, daily looking to the Cross for victory breeds total dependence upon the Lord, which is the idea all along. The Cross always humbles one, that is, if one is properly looking to the Cross. Works always bring about pride.

So, this is a constant, continuing exhibition of faith evidenced on the part of the believer, and it will never stop until the trump sounds.

HOW CAN I KNOW IF I AM IN LAW OR GRACE?

That is a good question!

Actually, the answer is simple. If you are walking in victory, you are walking in grace, i.e., the Cross. If you're failing, that means you are in law.

Now, by that, I am not teaching sinless perfection because the Bible does not teach such, but I am teaching that sin is not to have dominion over you as a believer. Paul said, *"For sin shall not have dominion over you: for you are not under the law, but under grace"* (Rom. 6:14).

Notice what he said: He did not say that there would never be a single sin committed again by the Christian who has proper faith in the proper means of victory, which is the Cross. Rather, he said that sin will not dominate us. In other words, the sin nature will not dominate the believer as it did before conversion.

What I am teaching is the simple truth of the Word of God, yet most believers have little understanding of the Cross, at least as it regards sanctification and what it realizes. As previously stated, this problem persists simply because almost all of the preaching and teaching in the last 40 years has been on faith, but for the most part, it has been faith in the wrong object, which is self. Consequently, this is faith that God will not honor.

So, the church has by and large been deprived of this great truth, with untold numbers now living a life of spiritual failure. This cannot be corrected until the church returns to the Cross and understands that great work not only for salvation but, as well, for sanctification. Actually, when writing his 14 epistles, Paul spent about 98 percent of his time explaining the Cross of Christ relative to sanctification. And yet, as stated, most believers have no idea of the part the Cross of Christ plays in the sanctification process.

ENTANGLED AGAIN

The phrase, *"And be not entangled again with the yoke of bondage,"* portrays the certain results of lawkeeping bondage. The word *entangled* in the Greek means "to be held within; to be ensnared."

It tells us the following: The Galatians had accepted Christ, and with that acceptance had come instantaneous and wonderful freedom. That means freedom to live a holy life, freedom to live as God wants one to live, and freedom to be what God wants one to be. However, now they were going back to law simply because some Jewish lawkeepers from Jerusalem were persuading them toward that direction. It was a giant step backward, even so far backward that it would be difficult to properly explain this wide chasm.

However, the reader may ask how the Galatians could go back into the law when, in fact, they had actually never been in the law of Moses previously. So, what does Paul mean?

That is certainly correct in that they had never known the law of Moses because they were Gentiles. They only became aware of this legalism as the Judaizers came after the church was already founded.

What Paul was saying is this: If they embarked upon a lifestyle of lawkeeping, even though it was the Mosaic law, failure would be the guaranteed result. This would be the same as if they went back to paganism from which they had been recently delivered.

Even though the law of Moses is in no way to be compared with paganistic laws, still, if one is looking for victory over sin from this source, or any source other than the Cross, he will have no more success than if he offered up sacrifice to idols. The end result will be the same in any case: failure.

ENTANGLEMENT

Entering into an effort of lawkeeping, and laws of any nature as we've already explained, can do nothing but conclude in defeat. So, the entanglement of which Paul speaks is actually the product of law, which is sin. Law was given to expose sin, in other words, to show man what he actually was and wasn't. So, the entanglement, as it refers to sin in this case, would put the Galatians right back where they were as pagans before they heard Paul preach the gospel. That should be a sobering thought.

That doesn't mean that the law of Moses was evil or bad. Not at all! Actually, the law contained righteousness, but the problem was, to attain to that righteousness, one had to keep the law perfectly, and I mean all of it, never failing even one time, which was and is impossible.

So, the law was meant to expose sin, to identify it, and to show man how inadequate that he is, which it did very, very well. It was never meant to save, never meant to give victory, and never meant to help one be an overcomer.

THE FOLLOWING QUESTION

Some may ask the question, why didn't God give man the strength and the power to keep the law?

He didn't for the following reason: Man's problem has always been pride. If God had made it possible for man to keep the law, he would have only been lifted up in pride, which would have made a bad matter worse. So, the law was given to show man how inadequate he was and is. As stated, it did that very well.

So, the reader is not to think that the law was bad, for it wasn't. It was just never meant to be used in the way that the Jews were trying to use it. What man needed, which was ultimately brought to pass, was what Jesus did at the Cross. In fact, everything about the law pointed to Christ and what He would do at Calvary. That included every sacrifice offered, and untold millions were offered down through the centuries.

When Christ came, He fulfilled the law in every capacity and in every respect. He did it by keeping the law perfectly and, as well, by addressing the broken law by giving Himself, as stated, as a sacrifice, which satisfied the demands of a thrice-holy God. While the Cross defeated Satan and all of his minions of darkness, the Cross, in essence, really did not have any-thing to do with the Evil One. It was to satisfy the demands of God, to settle a debt that man owed God but could not pay, and to atone for all sin, which Jesus did. This refers to sins of the past, the present, and the future—at least for all who will believe (Jn. 3:16). To be sure, when Jesus atoned for all sin, He defeated Satan in totality, but that was a by-product of the Cross and not the main thrust. The main thrust was to satisfy the demands of a thrice-holy God.

PAUL

"Behold, I Paul say unto you, that if you be circumcised, Christ shall profit you nothing" (Gal. 5:2).

The word *behold* or *look,* used as an introduction, is actually, "Mark my words!" It calls attention to what follows. If the Gala-tians allowed themselves to be circumcised, the result would be that Jesus Christ would profit them absolutely nothing at all. The phrase has the force of a deposition in a court of law.

Circumcision was, of course, the particular form of legalism that was a problem in Paul's day. The argument was simply that with circumcision having taken the position it had and signifying what it did, the choice was between Christ and no circumcision at all or circumcision and no Christ at all. In other words, God would put a minus sign before Christ in the lives of the Galatians if they put a plus sign before anything else.

This explains why Paul was so categorical in condemning the practice of circumcision for the Galatians. It was not that circumcision in itself was that important, for it wasn't. In fact, Paul himself had once had Timothy circumcised. Just four verses further on, he would declare that neither circumcision nor uncircumcision has any value. What Paul is condemning is the theology of circumcision, namely, the theology that makes works necessary for salvation and seeks to establish conformity to some external standards of behavior as a mark of spirituality.

NOTHING MUST COME BETWEEN THE BELIEVER AND CHRIST

In this verse the tense of the verb *to be circumcised* is important. It gives the sense, "If you should let yourself be circumcised." This implies quite clearly that the Galatians had not yet taken this step, but rather were considering it, and, therefore, their motivation became the important thing.

It also means that Paul was in no sense condemning those Jewish Christians, who had always, as it were, been circumcised. His advice to such is given in I Corinthians 7:17-20. If a man who has been circumcised becomes a Christian, he should remain circumcised, not seeking to change his status. If he is uncircumcised, he should remain uncircumcised. Once again, the point is that particular forms of legalism are not themselves the important issues. The issue is works versus grace, or as we will soon see, Spirit versus flesh. Paul's concern was that nothing could cloud perception of this central Christian doctrine.

As it regards the present time, or any time for that matter, anything that becomes the object of our faith instead of Christ and the Cross actually is sin simply because Paul also said, *"Whatsoever is not of faith is sin"* (Rom. 14:23).

For instance, there are many who think they can fast 21 days, or some such number, and this will give them victory over sin. It won't! There is only one thing that addresses sin, and that is the Cross. While fasting is certainly scriptural and will certainly be a blessing to the believer if engaged properly, it is not for the purpose of having victory over sin, and neither is anything else that one can name—only Christ and the Cross (I Cor. 1:17-18, 23; 2:2; Gal. 6:14; Col. 2:10-15).

THE HOLY SPIRIT SPEAKS THROUGH THE APOSTLE

The phrase, *"Behold, I Paul say unto you,"* presents the authority of the apostle.

This was Paul speaking to them—the one who had first preached the gospel to them, and who, before conversion, had, as well, submitted to circumcision. In addition, he was formerly a strenuous asserter of the necessity of observing the law of Moses. So, he was well acquainted with this of which he spoke.

In effect, the apostle was saying that if these Galatians were to be circumcised with a view to be justified by that, in whole or in part, such would amount to a rejection of the doctrine of justification by Christ, which would forfeit salvation if continued.

Jesus is to be a *whole Saviour.* In other words, He doesn't need any help. No one is to share with Him in the honor of saving men, and for all the obvious reasons. No rite, custom, or observance of law is to divide the honor with that which He produced at Calvary concerning His death.

As well, by him using his name here as he did, he is, in effect, telling the Galatians, "Don't listen to these false teachers who are attempting to lead you astray, but rather listen to me." Especially the manner in which he used his name: he is placing behind his statement the entirety of his faith—the Word of God on which he stands—and, in fact, everything in which he believes.

He does so because what he is saying is of great significance. It is a matter of life and death, or more importantly, a matter of the salvation or the loss of their souls. Nothing could be more important than that.

THE CONCLUSION OF HIS ARGUMENT

Paul concludes his argument of the entire epistle by describing the inescapable results of the Galatians submitting to the law. He names circumcision for the first time as the crux of the problem in Galatia. Acceptance of this requirement removes all the benefits of Christ and places upon the Galatians the burden of the whole law.

Thus, those sinning, and it is sin to place one's faith in something other than Christ and the Cross, would sever themselves from Christ and, thereby, fall from grace. By contrast, those living by faith have through the Holy Spirit the hope of righteousness. Actually, circumcision or uncircumcision, as stated, is not the issue with Paul. Rather, the deciding factor is faith operating through love, which is brought about by faith in

Christ and the Cross. In fact, this problem did not die with the Galatians. It is as prevalent now as then, or even more so. As previously stated, most Christians who are truly born again understand the Cross of Christ as it regards salvation; however, they understand it not at all as it regards sanctification, in other words, how we live for God on a daily basis.

Paul then asked who had torn up the race course, so to speak, on which they were running so well, and why their situation presently was losing its way. This action certainly could not have been the work of Christ, who had called them. It was rather an example of the way that evil spreads: *"a little leaven leavens the whole lump"* (Gal. 5:9).

The apostle expresses confidence that the Galatians would heed his concern and closes with a wish that their troublers, who, in essence, were the Judaizers, would leave them, and this false doctrine would come to a conclusion.

NO COMPROMISE

There can be no compromise between Christianity and Judaism, as there can be no compromise between Christ and what He has done for us at the Cross, and anything else that one might name. It doesn't matter what it is, how scriptural it might be in its own right, or how good it may seem to be on the surface. If it's not faith in Christ and what He has done for us at the Cross, it's faith that God will not recognize. The idea is that if you accept either one, you have to give up the other. Circumcision is a pledge or engagement to live by the rule of law, and that pretty well holds the case as it regards the present situation.

Going back to the Galatians, they were committing themselves to the practice of the whole law, and in that way alone, they would seek for justification. However, it should be remembered that in all the some 1,600 years of the law, not a single person other than the Lord Jesus Christ ever fully kept the law. With that in mind, one should tread carefully.

The believer should understand that we can be admitted into a state of righteousness only through the action of the Holy Spirit as we evidence faith in our Lord and what He did for us at Calvary. Consequently, the Christian owes the righteousness attributed to him, not to any type of works, ever how valuable they might be, but to a life of which faith is the motive. We speak of faith in Christ and the Cross, and love is the law.

THE TONE OF HIS STATEMENT

The whole tenor of the epistle shows that the apostle viewed the attempts of the Judaizing party, whomever they may have been, with indignation. At this point his language takes a more than usual stern and imperative tone. He speaks with the full weight, as stated, of his apostolic authority and warns the Galatians that no half measures will avail, but that they must decide once and for all either to give up Judaism or Christ. They cannot have both!

Galatians 5:2 is one of the passages that has been insisted upon as having a direct antagonism between Paul and the other apostles, but anyone who enters into the thought of the apostle and follows the course of his impassioned reasoning will see how false that charge is.

Even though he does speak sternly, still, due to that which is at stake—the eternal souls of men—sternness is called for at this time.

It must be understood that the meaning of the new covenant was given to the apostle Paul. Everything that the other apostles learned about it, they learned from Paul. In studying this for years, it seems to me that the only problem was the other apostles fully understanding that which the great apostle himself wrote in his 14 epistles. That's the reason that Peter said:

> And account that the longsuffering of our Lord is salvation; even as our beloved brother Paul also according to the wisdom given unto him has written unto you; as also in all his epistles, speaking in them of these things; in which are some things hard to be understood, which they that are unlearned and unstable wrest, as they do also the other Scriptures, unto their own destruction. You therefore, beloved, seeing you know these things before, beware lest you also, being led away with the error of the wicked, fall from your own steadfastness (II Pet. 3:15-17).

IF YOU BE CIRCUMCISED

The phrase, *"That if you be circumcised,"* presents a hypothetical case. The Galatians, as stated, had not yet submitted to that rite but were on the verge of doing so.

As certainly is obvious, Paul is not speaking of circumcision for health reasons, which would probably benefit every little baby boy. He is rather speaking of this particular rite with a view toward justification, in other words, that one had to do such in order to be saved, or as some taught it, to be a complete Christian. So, due to the fact that Galatians was written after the book of Acts, it seems that the church in Jerusalem was still producing some who claimed that *"except you be circumcised after the manner of Moses, you cannot be saved"* (Acts 15:1). The decision of James had been that the Gentiles were not to be troubled with the law (Acts 15:23-29).

However, inasmuch as James did not include the Jews in this statement, this, in effect, would ultimately destroy the Jewish segment of the church. James should have at that time taken a hard and fast position against law keeping among the Jews, as well, and, of course, we speak of those who had come to Christ. If it was the will of God for this stand to be taken as it regarded the Gentiles, and it definitely was, then it would have been the same toward the Jews. There aren't two ways of salvation and sanctification.

His not doing so at least encouraged the Judaizers to continue in this direction, which gave Paul so much trouble and threatened the early church as nothing else.

I'm not saying that James was directly involved in any of these situations, but rather that the position he took as recorded in Acts, Chapter 15, although favorable toward the Gentiles, was not the right decision regarding the Jews, which left them in a lawkeeping posture. This, no doubt, encouraged the Judaizers. To be sure, they caused Paul all types of difficulties and problems, with some of the churches on the verge of being lost because of this false direction.

CHRIST OR LAW?

The phrase, *"Christ shall profit you nothing,"* lays down the gauntlet that it must be one or the other—law or grace—it cannot be both! If the Galatians went in the direction of a dependence on circumcision, the fact is, it would amount to rejection of the Saviour and of the doctrine of justification by faith.

Paul is speaking here of much more than merely the method of living a Christian life and of growth in that life. While he certainly is addressing that throughout the entirety of this epistle, still, the entire tenor of his teaching is that if a person depends on anything else other than Christ for salvation, that person will be lost.

That is obvious as it regards the world, but many seek to deny such as it regards believers. Well, it just so happens that Paul is addressing nothing but believers in his epistle to the Galatians.

They had come to Christ by faith, which is the only manner in which one can come to Christ; however, they were now considering abandoning Christ in favor of the law.

IT IS EITHER CHRIST OR ETERNAL DAMNATION

Now, here is the catch: If the Galatians left Christ, thereby, going to the law, or anything else for that matter, they had reverted to the condition in which they were before salvation. Paul makes that very clear in Galatians 4:8.

Every sinner comes to salvation by faith, and that speaks of faith in Christ and His vicarious work at Calvary. Without such faith, it is impossible to be saved (Eph. 2:8-9).

If faith, after coming to Christ, is transferred from Christ to something else (in this case the law), the foundation of salvation has just been ripped apart. Actually, if the Cross is denied, the only thing left is law, but in modern times, a law of man's own devising. If it was by faith at the outset, that is at conversion, and if faith is demanded as we continue on with Christ, as it definitely is, if such faith in Christ is abandoned, that person reverts to a lost condition (Jn. 3:16; Eph. 2:8-9; Rev. 22:17).

It is Christ and the Cross and nothing but Christ and the Cross. That's the way it has always been, even from the time of Adam and Eve, and it will always be that way.

The tragedy is that these Galatians, even if they had embraced law, would not have considered in their own minds that they had forsaken Christ. That's the crux of the entire matter. This is what Paul is saying to them, but irrespective of what they thought, the fact would be that they would be forsaking Christ. This is the same thing for all others delving into other directions—laws of our own making.

The person who is depending on the Lord's Supper to save him in no way thinks in his mind that he has forsaken Christ. The same goes for water baptism, belonging to certain churches, etc. By adding these things to Christ, these individuals, as the Galatians of old, in no way consider themselves to be forsaking Christ, but rather the very opposite. However, the truth is, even as Paul here states, it is faith in Christ and Christ alone. Anything added to Him or taken from Him forfeits salvation.

FAITH IN CHRIST FOR SALVATION FAITH IN CHRIST FOR SANCTIFICATION

There are millions of Christians presently who maintain their faith in Christ for salvation but place it in something else altogether as it regards sanctification. In other words, there are many who think that if they fast so many days, this will give them victory as it regards living this life. They maintain their faith in Christ for salvation, but they do not maintain it for sanctification. This is the bane of the modern church. It understands the Cross of Christ relative to salvation but not at all as it regards sanctification.

The upshot is that the church staggers from one fad to the other. One year it is demons that need to be cast out of Christians; another year it is fasting; another year it is confession; another year it is the family curse, etc., etc.

While the things just named (and much that's not been named) may have some validity in their own respective ways, none of it will give one victory over the world, the flesh, and the Devil. It is imperative that the believer place his or her faith exclusively in Christ and what Christ has done for us at the Cross and maintain it there exclusively (Rom. 6:1-14; 8:1-11; I Cor. 1:17-18; 2:2; Gal. 6:14; Col. 2:10-15).

While these things mentioned, such as water baptism, etc., are not laws within themselves, we turn them into laws when we make them the object of our faith, which God can never sanction.

Very few modern Christians, as the Galatians of old, are reverting back to the law of Moses regarding circumcision, etc., but almost all are embracing things that never were intended by God to be embraced. What we are actually speaking of here is sin.

The modern church doesn't like to admit that the problem is sin, but that is the problem. There is only one solution for the problem of sin, and that is the Cross of Christ. That's where our Lord atoned for all sin—past, present, and future—at least for all who will believe (Jn. 3:16). That's where Satan and all of his minions of darkness were defeated. To be sure, the believer can have victory over sin only in one way, and that is by placing his or her faith exclusively in Christ and what Christ has done for us at the Cross, and maintain it exclusively in that finished work.

While fasting is definitely scriptural and will bless the believer if done in the right way, still, one can fast until he has almost starved himself to death and will find that the sin problem is still present when he begins to eat again. No, sin cannot be addressed in that fashion but only in the Cross of Christ.

So, we have two problems here:

1. We have multiple millions all over the world, even tens of millions, even hundreds of millions, who place their faith in something other than Christ and the Cross as it regards salvation. They think that by joining a church such saves them, or by doing good deeds, etc. It doesn't!

2. Then, we have untold millions of Christians who truly love the Lord. They are saved and Spirit-filled, but yet,

when it comes to sanctification, in other words, how we live this life, how we overcome, and how we have victory over the world, the flesh, and the Devil, their faith is in something other than Christ and the Cross. Consequently, even though they are saved, and many of them are used of God, still, there is no personal victory in their hearts and lives. In some way the sin nature is controlling such a person, and, regrettably, and as already stated, this includes almost all of the modern church.

As it regards the untold millions who think the church saves, or some such faith, let's see what Martin Luther said about this tragedy.

MARTIN LUTHER AND CATHOLICISM

The great Reformer, when addressing himself to this very verse (Gal. 5:2), was speaking of the religious organization to which he had once been associated and said:

Wherefore, this verse is a terrible thundering against all the kingdom of the pope. For all the priests, monks, and nuns, who live in their cloisters (I speak of the best of them) repose all their trust and their confidence in their own works, righteousness, vows and merits, and not in Christ, whom they most wickedly and blasphemously imagine to be an angry judge, an accuser, and condemner; and, there-fore, in this verse, they hear their judgment that Christ profits them nothing."

He then said: "What profit can they have by His death and blood shedding, by His resurrection, victory over sin, death, and the Devil, seeing they are able to overcome these monsters by their own strength? And what tongue can express, or what heart can conceive how horrible a thing it is to make Christ unprofitable."

The Reformer continued to say, "It appears sufficiently that nothing under the sun is more hurtful than the doctrine of man's traditions and works; for they utterly abolish and overthrow the truth of the gospel, the true worshipping of God, and Christ Himself, in whom the Father has ordained all things. Wherefore, all that are either the authors or maintainers of the doctrine of works are oppressors of the gospel; they make the death and victory of Christ unprofitable, blemish and deface His sacraments, and take away the true use thereof; and are blasphemers, enemies and deniers of God, and of all His promises and benefits."

FORFEITURE OF SALVATION

We may compare this verse with the awful passage of Hebrews 10:26-30, referring to the consequences accruing to Jewish Christians because of their relapsing to Judaism. It is difficult to overestimate the importance of this passage in determining the relationship between trust in Christ's atonement and participation in the benefits of that atonement. It is at his extreme peril that a Christian allows himself misgivings as to whether Christ's mediation is all sufficient for the securing of his peace with God and his part in God's kingdom.

It is by reliance upon Christ's Word that our salvation through Christ is secured. By distrust in it, our salvation is brought into peril. By definite unbelief, our salvation is forfeited. This is in perfect accordance with the apostolic doctrine in general, but rarely is it so strongly and incisively asserted as it is here.

One who relies on his or her efforts to keep the law is not relying on Christ. In fact, Paul says that Jesus is of no value at all to such a person. God's Word itself is without value to the hearer unless it is combined with faith (Heb. 4:2). The external ceremonies of Israel's old way are of no value to those whose hearts are to be strengthened by grace, and can only be strengthened by grace (Heb. 13:9).

As Scripture strips away the religious crutches that people depend on, it is good to note that God has provided all we need for salvation, growth, and meaningful life in Jesus Christ (Col. 2:9-19).

A PERSONAL TESTIMONY

Sometime back, I received a letter from a dear lady who had just given her heart to Christ as a result of our telecast.

She related how that she was a member of one of the Baptist churches in her city and had been for many, many years. She went on to state how that she was so acquainted with Baptist doctrine that she taught the new converts class. She stated how that she was a part of every program in the church, even to the place of neglecting her family. However, in listening to the message over television that Sunday morning, the Holy Spirit began to convict her heart, and she realized that for all of her religiosity, she really wasn't saved. She prayed with me, and the Spirit of God touched her heart and in a few moments, she knew that she was now born again.

Tragically and sadly, there are untold millions in the same condition as this dear lady. She was religious. She had saturated herself with good works. No one would have ever looked at her and thought that she was unsaved, but her own heart told her that she was unsaved when the Spirit of God began to move as the Word of God was preached. Sadly, as previously stated, this is the condition of untold millions.

I TESTIFY

"For I testify again to every man who is circumcised, that he is a debtor to do the whole law" (Gal. 5:3).

Paul has already given one good reason the Galatians should remain firm in the freedom that Christ has given them. Now he will give another. The two reasons are:

1. To fall into the practice of circumcision, or any other form of works we might quickly add, is to lose the value of Christ's death, both for salvation and for living the Christian life.

2. To choose circumcision or anything else other than Christ and the Cross, at least as it refers to legalism, is,

in fact, to choose legalism. Consequently, such a direction involves taking on the burden of the whole law. It must be understood that there is only one person who has ever kept the whole law and that was the Lord Jesus Christ. This means that the pickings are slim, to use the vernacular.

Had the legalizers (Judaizers) warned the Galatians that this was involved? One is inclined to doubt it, feeling rather that they were slyly proceeding step-by-step in their efforts to impose legalistic religion—first the feast (Gal. 4:10), then circumcision, and eventually the whole law of Moses.

So, the reader will understand that none of this means that the law of Moses was bad. In fact, the law was from God and was holy and right, but only in its place and during its time.

In fact, the law was never meant to save and was never meant to give victory. It told man what he must do but gave him no power to do it.

The law ever pointed to Christ, and when He came, He fulfilled all of the law, which made it now unnecessary. In fact, the prophets had predicted the ending of the law and the advent of a new covenant, which, of course, Jesus brought and actually was (Isa. 42:6; 49:8; 55:3; 59:21; 61:8; Jer. 31:31-34; Heb. 8:6-13; 10:16; 12:24; 13:20).

What's the point of keeping feast days when the one to whom they pointed has now come? What's the point of keeping the Sabbath when that particular law referred to the rest that would come in Jesus? Why offer up more sacrifices when the principle sacrifice has now come and been offered?

To attempt to keep something that has already been fulfilled is bad enough, but to claim that the doing of such is necessary for salvation or victory in Christ is adding insult to injury. As stated, such attitude is saying what Jesus did at Cavalry is not enough. Irrespective, the law could not save anyway and never was meant by God to do so.

TO EVERY MAN THAT IS CIRCUMCISED

The phrase, *"For I testify again to every man who is circumcised,"* refers to the fact that Paul had told them of all of these things when he was with them in the founding of these churches.

He who allows himself to be circumcised, at least as it refers here to the Mosaic law, thereby, commits himself wholly to the law, just as it might be said that he who places his faith entirely in Christ and the Cross commits himself wholly to Christ.

In fact, the act of circumcision placed a man under the legal system of Moses just as the act of water baptism places one under the Christian system, at least as far as outward show is concerned. From that time forward, he could not choose one part and refuse another but was bound alike by all.

As is obvious, verse 3 continues the argument of verse 2. Not only would the Galatians lose the aid of the Holy Spirit in the living of their Christian lives, that is, if they did this thing, they would also be assuming the burden of the entire legalistic system. Paul warns them that the acceptance of circumcision would be in principle the acceptance of the whole of that system.

The fact that the apostle points this out to the Galatians probably implies that the Judaizers had not related this to them. They were now asking the Galatian Christians (or demanding them) to accept circumcision as a rite by which they would then become sons of Abraham and thus participants in the blessing of the Abrahamic covenant, which can actually only be done in Christ and not keeping of law.

TO DO THE WHOLE LAW

The phrase, *"That he is a debtor to do the whole law,"* refers to one who is under obligation—one who is bound to do a certain thing.

The obligation is as the context shows, one which the Christian must not assume, not the least being that one could lose his soul. The believer is free from the law in three respects:

1. He is free from the condemnation that imposes upon the one who would disobey it. As we have previously said, the moral part of the law of Moses is still incumbent upon the entirety of the world. Even though the unsaved do not realize such, they are answerable to this standard of morality given by God. Some would ask, "Well, isn't the believer answerable to the moral law?" Of course, all of us are answerable to the standard of righteousness that God has imposed, and rightly so, but the keeping of the law, the keeping of it perfectly, was all done in Christ. Our faith in Him makes us lawkeepers instead of lawbreakers. Also, He took its penalty on the

Cross, i.e., its condemnation; consequently, my trust in Him means that I am no longer under its condemnation. However, I will say again that all are under its condemnation who have not accepted Christ. Christ alone can save one from the broken law.

2. The believer is free from the law as a means of justification, and this is extremely important. Justification through the law, which actually could not be done, demanded perfect obedience. Because perfect obedience was literally impossible, justification by this route was impossible as well. In today's language, it means that no one can be justified by works, which is the very ways and means attempted by the world. For instance, when Mother Theresa died, the whole world lauded her for the simple reason that such is their model of justification. In other words, her good works made her a saint or earned her salvation, or whatever terminology those in that capacity might use. I do not personally judge the woman because I did not know her heart; however, if the things she said are any type of indication, she was not saved, and neither is anyone else who trusts in works.

3. The believer is free from the obligation to render obedience to its statutes. The reason is simple, and as we have already stated, Jesus has already done this for us, actually, in our place as the true man, and our faith in Him grants us His victory. It is the Holy Spirit within us who helps us to keep the moral law, and He does so without it becoming a problem of any nature. In fact, the demands of the

Holy Spirit are far more than the demands of the law ever generated. However, whatever He demands of us, He also gives us the power to do it. I never think about the law simply because the Holy Spirit is guiding me in all that I do. When we follow His direction, every moral precept is obeyed without it even being addressed at all.

THE LAW AND THE BELIEVER

By what rule can one isolate certain parts of the Old Testament law as binding upon Christians and disregard other parts as purely Jewish in their application? Neither the Galatians nor any other believer is obligated to obey any of the law; however, submission of the Galatians to the rite of circumcision makes them a party to the covenant of the law, and the law requires from everyone thus committed a full and perfect obedience.

Wuest says, "The ethics of the Pauline epistles, and the ministry of the Holy Spirit, take the place of and are a vast improvement upon the Mosaic law. Actually, it is an improvement in every respect."

Whatever is of value for the church as it regards the ethics of the law is found in the passages of the New Testament epistles.

That is not to say, however, that the great principles of conduct underlying the statutes of the Mosaic law are to be ignored, as should be obvious. The Old Testament, even though superseded by the New Testament, which is specially designed for the church, has great value for us presently. Still, it must be used with the following two guiding principles in mind:

1. The law was specially adapted to the needs of the nation of Israel and for the time before the Cross. We must not forget that.

2. Its legal enactments, where they deal with general principles of conduct that are universal and eternal in their application, must never be treated as legally binding upon the believer, but only as ethics to guide our conduct. While the believer definitely does keep the moral law, still, it is not done as a legality but as a matter of faith in Christ. Christ is the true man, and as such, our faith in Him makes us true men as well.

WHAT DO WE ACTUALLY MEAN BY FAITH IN HIM?

Every true believer claims faith in Christ, which, in fact, they had to have in order to be saved; however, I am persuaded that most believers do not exactly know what that means as it regards having faith in Him. I suspect that if pressed for an answer, most would simply say that they trust Christ as it regards their salvation. They believe in Him. They believe that He is the Son of God and that He died on Calvary in order that we might be saved.

All of that is correct and right, at least as far as it goes; however, the main theme of the finished work of Christ is actually not dealing with initial salvation, but rather with our continued walk with God. As Paul has said, some begin in the Spirit, which means they trust Christ, with the Holy Spirit then bringing them to salvation (Gal. 3:3). But now, they try to maintain their walk before God by resorting to law, which throws them into the flesh, which means the Holy Spirit will not help us in that erroneous way because it is not God's way.

THE CROSS

The idea of having faith in Christ is faith in what He did at Calvary. As we have stated repeatedly, He paid the sin debt, which broke the grip of sin. Consequently, the believer's continual trust in the Cross of Christ guarantees the keeping of all of these particular moral commandments; however, as stated, such is not done in the realm of legalities, in other words, "I must not steal, I must not bear false witness," etc. Such is doomed to failure.

Once we are properly in Christ, which all of us are at salvation, and we continue to trust Him on a daily basis by taking up the Cross and all of its benefits, the believer automatically keeps the commandments (Lk. 9:23). To use some modern vernacular, it's a done deal.

The moment the believer throws himself into the legal mode, which means that he has got to try to obey the commandments, he is doomed to failure because he has reverted to law.

Look at it this way: These things are not something we must do; it is something that has already been done—done by Christ. Properly in Him, they are done within our lives as well.

No believer should ever get up each morning and think within himself, "I've got to keep the Ten Commandments; I've got to obey God," etc. That's not the idea at all, and such a course will only lead to failure simply because the believer, as stated, has now reverted to law. The believer doesn't even actually have to think of these things. We are in Christ. Our trust is in what He did at the Cross, which carries its benefits to me even on an hourly basis, and the Holy Spirit guarantees it done (Rom. 6:1-14; 8:1-11; I Cor. 1:17-18, 23; 2:2; Gal. 6:14; Col. 2:10-15).

There is no struggle, no fight, and no self-effort, with the exception of continued faith in the Cross of Christ.

Martin Luther said, "Therefore it is most true that they who do the law, do it not, for the more they go about to fulfill the law, the more they transgress it."

THE BELIEVER AND JESUS

The key to all of this, of course, is Jesus. Our proper relationship with Him guarantees a victorious, overcoming Christian life. As well, it guarantees a life that is *"joy unspeakable and full of glory"* (I Pet. 1:8). It is the most fulfilling, rewarding, joyful, and exuberant life that one could ever know (Jn. 10:10). And yet, many believers, and I think possibly most, do not have that joy and that peace even though they actually do have salvation.

They are failing in some particular aspect of their moral lives, and despite all of their efforts to cease and desist this which has put them in bondage, the situation is getting worse rather than getting better.

You see, our mistake is this: We think that if we can just quit doing this thing, whatever it might be, our troubles will then be over. So, we set about with all of our efforts and strength to stop the infraction, the sin, whatever; however, the stopping of this thing is not really the problem or the answer. To be frank, the sin or the failure is actually only a symptom of the real problem.

WHAT IS THE REAL PROBLEM?

The real problem is that we are not properly trusting Christ.

Let's look at that for a moment. The Bible really has very few formulas, and for the obvious reasons. However, I think that which I am about to give will be sanctioned and is sanctioned by the Holy Spirit. The road to victory is the following:

- Jesus Christ is the source of all that we receive from God (Jn. 1:1-3, 14, 20, 29).
- The Cross of Christ is the means and the only means for us to receive these good things (Rom. 6:1-14; I Cor. 1:17-18, 23; 2:2).
- The Cross of Christ must ever be the object of our faith, with us understanding that it was there that every price was paid and every debt settled (Gal. 6:14; Col. 2:10-15).
- We must understand that Christ is the source and the Cross is the means, and the Cross of Christ must ever be the object of our faith. With this understanding, then the Holy Spirit can begin to work in our lives. He works entirely within the framework of the Cross, which means that the Cross gave and gives Him the legal means to do all that He does. We will then know victory in our lives simply because the Holy Spirit will be doing what

needs to be done, and it will not be us attempting to do such in the flesh (Rom. 8:1-11; Eph. 2:13-18).

If we follow the guidelines laid down, we will then be properly trusting Christ. If the believer doesn't function according to the diagram laid down above, he will find that the sin nature is once again ruling him.

NOW LET'S LOOK AT THE SIN NATURE

The sin nature is simply the evil nature that came to man after the fall in the garden of Eden. In other words, his entire nature became that of sin and that of transgression. Due to the fact that all of humanity, theoretically speaking, was in the loins of Adam, whatever he did passed to the entirety of the human race. His divine nature before the fall was lost at the fall and was replaced by the evil nature, which is the cause of all the problems in the world. As stated, unsaved man is ruled by the sin nature.

Upon coming to Christ, while the sin nature is not removed, one might say that it is, however, disconnected, so to speak. It's not a physical thing, as should be obvious, but rather that which is spiritual. That's the reason Paul said, *"How shall we, who are dead to sin, live any longer therein"* (Rom. 6:2).

In fact, in Romans, Chapter 6, if the reader will substitute *sin nature* every time the word *sin* is used, the entirety of the treatment of this chapter will become clearer. If one is to notice, the apostle did not say that the sin nature is dead, but rather that the believer is dead to the sin nature, or is supposed to be.

That's what I mean by it being disconnected. Remember, he is addressing believers.

HOW IS THE SIN NATURE REACTIVATED?

Failing the Lord, in other words sinning, does not reactivate the sin nature. What reactivates the sin nature in the life of the Christian is the following: When the believer fails the Lord, which means to sin in some way, he automatically sets about to see to it that it doesn't happen again. This is where the problem begins most of the time. Instead of placing his faith exclusively in Christ and the Cross, he places it in something else. It may be fasting, memorizing Scripture, or whatever; however, if it's not faith in Christ and the Cross, such direction actually constitutes spiritual adultery. In other words, one is not being faithful to Christ.

FAITHFUL TO CHRIST

When the believing sinner comes to Christ, he is, in essence, married to Christ (Rom. 7:1-4; II Cor. 11:1-4). This means that Christ is meant to meet our every need and, in fact, is the only one who can meet our every need. He does so through what He accomplished at the Cross, with our faith anchored securely in that finished work. Then the Holy Spirit will help us grandly.

However, when we place our faith in something else, no matter what it is, that is constituted as spiritual adultery, and then the sin nature is reactivated, so to speak. Due to the fact that most of the modern church little understands the Cross of Christ and sanctification—actually not understanding it at all—this means that the sin nature rules in almost all of these hearts and lives. The people are saved, Spirit-filled, and even used by the Lord, but they do not have victory within their hearts and within their lives.

Paul said, *"For sin shall not have dominion over you: for you are not under the law, but under grace"* (Rom. 6:14).

If it were not possible for the sin nature to dominate a believer, why would the apostle have said such a thing?

We must never forget that the Cross of Christ alone answers the sin question. When we try to address it any way other than by the Cross, we fail, and the situation steadily becomes worse. It is always, *"Jesus Christ, and Him crucified"* (I Cor. 2:2).

THE OBJECT OF FAITH

When we simply place our faith in Christ and His victory afforded by the Cross—and I speak of victory as it regards our everyday walk before God—the Holy Spirit then steps in with His power, and victory is assured.

I pray that the reader does not weary of this constant repetition in this fashion, but the truth is, we are addressing the single most important thing as it regards the child of God—victory in his or her heart and life. This is the greatest area of conflict and an area, I think I can say without fear of contradiction, where most Christians are failing. As I have repeatedly said, there has been very little preaching regarding the Cross in the last few decades; consequently, these great truths, which are really the bedrock of the Word of God, have gradually slipped away from the church.

FREE

The following is where the believer is in Christ, which is guaranteed by the Holy Spirit, that is, if we properly trust in Christ and the Cross: *"There is therefore now no condemnation to them which are in Christ Jesus, who walk not after the flesh, but after the Spirit. For the law* (God's law of victory) *of the Spirit of life* (the Holy Spirit) *in Christ Jesus* (which is given by and through Christ Jesus) *has made me free from the law of sin and death"* (Rom. 8:1-2).

The reason I repeat these things is simply because they must get down into a person's spirit before that person can actually realize what is being said. A mere mental affirmation will not accomplish this task. In fact, millions believe, but it is only in their heads and not really in their hearts. If the reader can have these truths constantly given to him, after awhile, they will begin to connect.

Looking at the Gospels and the repetition given there, and looking at Paul as he says the same thing over and over, sometimes in different ways, we realize why the Holy Spirit is doing this. These truths, as stated, must get down into our spirits, and they can only do such by faith and us constantly hearing them over and over again.

It may be at morn, when the day is awaking,
When sunlight through darkness and shadow is breaking
That Jesus will come in the fullness of glory,
To receive from the world His own.

It may be at midday, it may be at twilight,
It may be, perchance that the blackness of midnight,
Will burst into light in the blaze of His glory,
When Jesus receives His own.

While hosts cry Hosanna! from heaven descending,
With glorified saints and the angels attending,
With grace on His brow, like a halo of glory,
Will Jesus receive His own.

Oh, joy, oh, delight! should we go without dying;
No sickness, no sadness, no dread, and no crying;
Caught up through the clouds with our Lord into glory,
When Jesus receives His own.

THE YOKE OF BONDAGE

CHAPTER 2

FALLEN FROM GRACE

CHAPTER TWO

FALLEN FROM GRACE

"CHRIST IS BECOME OF NO EFFECT unto you, whosoever of you are justified by the law; you are fallen from grace" (Gal. 5:4).

THE FORFEITURE OF CHRIST

Once again Paul reiterates his point, this time dropping the hypothetical "if" for the much stronger statement: *"Christ is become of no effect unto you, whosoever of you are justified by the law* (you who are trying to be justified by the law have been alienated from Christ)*; you are fallen from grace* (you have fallen away from grace)."

Have they desired to be saved by legalism? In that case, Christ is of no value to them, and the burden of keeping the whole law is theirs. This, of course, is a fruitless task, in other words, impossible.

The phrase, *"Christ is become of no effect unto you,"* presents a powerful statement. He is stressing again the full implications of what he has said.

The Judaizers taught that only by keeping the law was it possible to be justified before God. Paul used a very strong Greek verb, prefaced by a preposition, to stress that all who wish to be justified by the law were totally cut off from Christ; they had fallen out of grace. Consequently, if they remained in this condition, they had absolutely no hope of salvation.

Some have claimed that Paul is referring here not to the justification of these Galatians, but rather to their sanctification, i.e., their walk before God as it pertains to victory. That is true as the overall character of this epistle is concerned; however, he is dealing directly with their salvation in this passage, even as the next phrase tells us. So, he is warning them that this foray into legalism will not only destroy their victorious walk in Christ but, as well, will ultimately cause them to lose their souls. In fact, it's not possible to derive anything else from this Scripture.

The actual rendering of the phrase, *"Christ is become of no effect unto you,"* literally says, "You were (are more idiomatically) abolished, made nothing from Christ." This is a condensed form of expression for "you are made nothing (unchristianized) and cut off from Christ. Your relations to Christ are canceled, and you are Christians no longer."

JUSTIFIED BY THE LAW

The phrase, *"whosoever of you are justified by the law,"* actually says, "Whosoever of you who attempt to be justified by the law." It is obvious here that he is speaking of justification, which pertains to salvation rather than sanctification.

So, Paul here poses a juxtaposition—the act or an instance of placing two or more things side by side. He places law and grace side by side, telling the Galatians that they cannot have both. It is either grace or law.

If, in fact, the believer attempts to harbor some law, even as he will later say concerning the leaven, ultimately, the law will completely root out grace until there is nothing left but law, which causes the person to be eternally lost.

It's like putting a rotten apple in a barrel of good apples. The good apples will not make the rotten apple good, but rather the rotten apple will ultimately corrupt the good apples. Justification by law—obedience in this section—is contrasted with righteousness by faith—acceptance. The words "justified by law" contrast, therefore, with "righteousness by faith." The power energizing the one is man's will; that energizing the other is the Holy Spirit.

In the strongest language possible, Paul states, as we shall see in the next phrase, the consequences of seeking to be justified by the law.

THE ABANDONING OF GRACE

It is important to see that this loss (or potential loss) was due to the fact that they had abandoned God's grace, or were considering doing so by their actions, and not because God had taken it away. The two ways are absolutely incompatible. The apostasy of turning to the law is fatal, which the apostle is here forcibly bringing out (Heb. 10:26-31).

There was in Galatia the possibility of apostasy, which the apostle is here addressing. The Galatians had experienced grace but were now turning from God. Since New Testament times, it has been beyond comprehension how those who have *"tasted of the heavenly gift, and were made partakers of the Holy Spirit, and have tasted the good Word of God, and the powers of the world to come"* (Heb. 6:4-5), could return to the old life of law.

This question has been so acute that some have developed a theology that denies its possibility. They say that any who return permanently to the life of sin never have found new life in Christ to begin with, and all who have found such life, if temporarily losing their way, will inevitably come back to their Father and home. While it is certainly true that those in this condition can come back anytime they so desire, they cannot come back if they insist on continuing in law.

Others more boldly insist that once a man becomes a child of God, his choices and decisions cannot alter this new relationship, but neither Scripture nor human experience substantiates such teaching.

GOD'S SELF-LIMITATION

This false theology (and false it is) is built on a minimizing of the power of man's satanic adversary and on a gross misunderstanding of the power of God.

One of the most sublime truths of the New Testament revelation is that of God's self-limitation. He will not transgress or abuse human freedom. The same God who will not save a man against his will, will not keep a man saved against his will. This is the key to sustaining grace. As long as a soul desires and wills to serve and love God, he is secure, but when a man chooses to return to the slavery of sin and Satan, God almighty will respect that decision. However, the person will be eternally lost, that is, if he remains in that condition.

ISRAEL

In fact, this is the very reason that Israel fell, which has caused untold millions of Jews to be eternally lost. Paul said of them, *"For they* (Israel) *being ignorant of God's righteousness, and going about to establish their own righteousness* (attempting to do so through the law)*, have not submitted themselves unto the righteousness of God"* (Rom. 10:3).

In fact, that's why they crucified Christ. Actually, the law will always crucify Christ because its penalty is death. So, if one attempts to justify oneself by works of any nature, he is at the same time denying the justification afforded by Christ, which alone God will accept. He (man) is thereby lost. In fact, grace righteousness and legal righteousness cannot coexist.

Jesus said of the Holy Spirit, *"And when He* (the Holy Spirit) *is come, He will reprove the world of sin, and of righteousness, and of judgment."*

He then said, *"Of sin, because they believe not on Me* (believe that I can cleanse from sin and bestow righteousness)*."*

Then He said, *"Of righteousness, because I go to My Father, and you see Me no more."* This means that His spotless righteousness, which He had won and purchased by His perfect life, and more particularly His death, was accepted by His Father. God could not accept man's righteousness in any capacity, but He did accept that provided by His Son. This is referred to as the righteousness of God, which is actually saying, "the righteousness that is of God," meaning that it is not of man.

Last of all, Jesus said, *"Of judgment, because the prince of this world is judged"* (Jn. 16:8-11). This means that if men do not accept the righteousness of God, they will experience the judgment of God—the same judgment that's already being passed upon Satan, which is recorded in Revelation 20:10-15. So, it's the righteousness of God or eternal hell! It is just that clear and plain.

FALLEN FROM GRACE

The phrase, *"you are fallen from grace,"* refers to apostatizing.

The word *fallen* in the Greek is *ekplpto* and means, "to drop away, to cast out, to fall away." The word *grace* is *charis* and means, "the divine influence on the heart, and its reflection in the life."

So, if one falls, which one will if one forsakes grace, there remains no other way to be saved. In fact, the writer of Hebrews said, *"For it is impossible … If they shall fall away, to renew them again unto repentance; seeing they crucify to themselves the Son of God afresh, and put Him to an open shame"* (Heb. 6:4-6).

The Holy Spirit is not saying here that a backslider cannot come back to God, but that one cannot come back if he refuses to come God's way. God's way is the way of faith, which refers to faith in Christ and what He did for us at the Cross.

The book of Hebrews was written primarily to Jews who had accepted Christ but now, because of discouragement and persecution, were thinking of going back into the law, or else, had already done so.

When they began to offer up sacrifices again, they were actually crucifying in *"themselves the Son of God afresh,"* which put *"Him to an open shame,"* meaning that they were publically rejecting His sacrificial offering on Calvary. Of course, for those who had done this terrible thing, if they had repented of it and, thereby, renounced it to come back to Christ, they would have been instantly forgiven and restored. However, if they insisted upon remaining in that situation, then their situation was exactly as the apostle said: impossible.

These are dreadful sentences against the righteousness of the law and man's own righteousness.

This, then, is the final conclusion: Either one must forego Christ or the righteousness of the law. If one retains Christ, then one is righteous before God, but if one remains with the law, Christ avails him nothing. With that being the case, one is bound to keep the whole law, which is impossible, and will come under its sentence, which says, *"Cursed be he who confirms* (cursed is everyone who fulfills) *not all the words of this law* (things that are written in this law) *to do them"* (Deut. 27:26).

MAN'S TRADITIONS

When we speak of the law of Moses, we are, at the same time, speaking of man's traditions. This means, in the words of

Martin Luther, "Either the pope with his religious rabble must reject all those things wherein hitherto they have put their trust, or else Christ cannot be profitable to them."

When Paul says, *"You are fallen from grace,"* he means that you are no longer in the kingdom of grace.

This statement must be carefully considered, for it is of great importance. He who falls from grace utterly loses the atonement, the forgiveness of sins, and the righteousness, liberty, and life that Jesus Christ has merited for us by His death and resurrection. Instead, one purchases to himself the wrath and judgment of God, which is sin, death, and bondage of the Devil, along with damnation, which must come upon all of those who are not under grace.

Indeed, this of which Paul says, and which the Holy Spirit told him to say, often terrifies the enemies of faith and grace, that is to say, all who seek righteousness by works. As it refers to the traditions of men, this also means that all who are trusting in their church to save them are, in fact, eternally lost. This includes the ordinances of the church, such as water baptism, the Lord's Supper, tongues, or works of any kind. One cannot trust Christ and works at the same time.

ITS WORTH REPEATING

Churches are full of people who are putting their faith in works rather than in Christ, which is why the following story bears repeating.

A dear lady wrote and told me how she had been a member of the Baptist church all of her life. She stated that she knew

Baptist doctrine inside and out and, in fact, knew this doctrine so well that she served in her church as a teacher of the new convert's class. She said, "Brother Swaggart, last Sunday morning I began to watch the telecast, and for the first time in my life, I sensed the convicting power of the Holy Spirit in my heart. All of a sudden, I realized that even though I was very religious, I was not, in fact, saved."

She then went on to say how that she prayed with me and gave her heart and life to the Lord Jesus Christ.

It took something for this woman to admit this. In fact, she could not have been brought to this place of revelation without the power of the Holy Spirit working upon God's Word, revealing this truth to her.

However, let me quickly add that she happened to be Baptist, but it could and does, in fact, apply to anyone.

DECEPTION

How is it that this woman, who actually taught a class in her church, could be so deceived?

In fact, there are untold millions who are in the same condition. The truth is, the only true way salvation can be presented and understood is for it to be preached under the anointing of the Holy Spirit, with the convicting power of the Holy Spirit then working on the heart of the listener (Jn. 16:8-11).

Sadly, most preachers do not preach under any anointing of the Holy Spirit. In fact, most do not even believe in the anointing. It must ever be understood that the Word separated from the Spirit cannot effect any change. Also, it must be understood that just because it is the Word of God, it does not necessarily mean that the Holy Spirit is anointing it. Jesus said, *"The Spirit of the Lord is upon Me, because He has anointed Me to preach the gospel to the poor"* (Lk. 4:18). There are many preachers who are preaching the gospel, even preaching it truthfully, but they do not have the anointing of the Holy Spirit.

Why?

Most have not been baptized with the Holy Spirit as recorded in Acts 2:4, and sad to say, most who have little rely on Him for that which He alone can do. Some few do, but most don't.

GRACE AND SIN

Incidentally, people who sin and subsequently repent do not fall from grace, but those people who willfully turn from the grace of God, which comes only through Christ, have definitely fallen from grace. We speak of those who have changed the object of their faith from Christ and Him crucified to something else, and it doesn't really matter what the something else actually is. Such individuals can seek forgiveness and come back if they so desire. If not, however, they will be eternally lost. God does not provide grace in any other way except through the Cross of Christ.

Many believers are fond of saying about other people, "He (or she) is fallen." It should be understood that no one is fallen from grace who continues to trust Christ. If that was not the case, that would mean that every single person is fallen from grace.

All sin is terrible, but God will always forgive it if the person will turn to Him in humility and confess the sin and seek forgiveness.

The Scripture plainly says, *"If we confess our sins, He is faithful and just to forgive us our sins, and to cleanse us from all unrighteousness"* (I Jn. 1:9). As well, the Lord does not put a limit on how many times He will forgive.

Some Christians are fond of talking about the God of the second chance. While that certainly is true, He is also the God of the third chance, and the fifth, the hundredth, and thousandth for that matter. One must not limit the grace of God. Of course, no Christian wants to sin, with that terrible malady being repugnant to the heart and life of the believer. Yet, many Christians seem to enjoy limiting grace to others while wanting no such limitations on themselves. But I suspect that such attitude stems from self-righteousness more than anything else.

For a person to be fallen, even as Paul here describes, that person must forsake Christ and no longer trust Him and, thereby, trust something else. He is then fallen. However, as long as anyone trusts Christ, God will never turn that person away but will always accept him with open arms. To trust Christ means that irrespective of the failure, he continues to come to Christ for mercy and grace and seeks that which the Cross alone provides. For instance, Simon Peter failed, but he didn't fall. Judas, on the other hand, did fall and, in fact, never sought mercy or grace and, thereby, died, sad to say, eternally lost.

However, the idea is not constant repentance and forgiveness, as wonderful as forgiveness is, but rather victory over sin. That is what Paul is teaching here in this epistle, which can only come by the means of the Cross.

THROUGH THE SPIRIT

"For we through the Spirit wait for the hope of righteousness by faith" (Gal. 5:5).

The essence of the gospel is now brought forward in the last full statement of the principle of justification by faith as Paul here states the case. Up to this point, the apostle has been talking only of the Galatians, using the pronoun *you*. However, we should understand that he is referring to all believers and for all time as well.

He has been warning them about what they seem to be doing. Now the pronoun changes to "we" and is placed in an emphatic position. It is as if Paul is saying, "But we Christians do not choose legalism; rather, we wait in faith through the Holy Spirit for the full realization of God's righteousness." In fact, each word in this verse is extremely important and, except for the non-theological words, has already been defined. After "we," which is prominent in the Greek text, comes the first of these words:

• *"Through the Spirit."* This is a reminder that the Holy Spirit will only function from the foundation of faith, and faith, we might quickly add, that is centered in the Cross. He will not function in the realm of law, etc.

- *"By faith."* This is the key word and stands in contrast to flesh, as all should be aware from the arguments as already given by the apostle. Circumcision is of the flesh. Faith denotes an entirely different approach.
- *"Wait"* (or waits eagerly). This refers to the Christian waiting for the full realization of salvation, which will come at the resurrection. He does not work for it; he waits for it.
- *"The hope of righteousness."* The righteousness for which we hope does not refer to that imputed righteousness the believer already has through faith in Christ's death, but rather refers to the completed righteousness that will come when the resurrection takes place. In the Bible, *hope* refers to that which, though certain, is not yet fully realized.

I inserted "faith" before the "hope of righteousness" simply because faith must come before such hope can be realized.

THROUGH THE HOLY SPIRIT

The phrase, *"for we through the Spirit,"* emphasizes the pronoun *we* and thus says that he—Paul—and those following him are living through (by means of) the Spirit. Although it is unstated, those who are under the law live by means of the flesh—their reliance is upon the flesh instead of the Holy Spirit. Consequently, they are doomed to failure as the one depending on the Spirit is guaranteed success. We are now speaking of two things:

1. Paul is speaking of salvation by faith, the initial experience of one coming to Christ. The Holy Spirit anoints the preacher to preach the Word. He then anoints the Word as it goes to its intended destination. The Holy Spirit then seizes the sinner with conviction, making him realize his need for salvation, which can only come through Christ. The sinner is then arrested, if you will, and brought to Christ, and upon an exhibition of faith in Christ, which is also supplied by the Spirit, the sinner is saved and becomes a new creation in Christ Jesus. Even though Jesus Christ is the one who made all of this possible, it is the Holy Spirit who superintends all that is done, hence, through the Spirit.

2. It is only through the Spirit, which I have been relating over and over again, that one can have a victorious, overcoming Christian life. I am speaking of victory over sin and the powers of darkness. The Spirit of God works only as it regards the righteousness of God, which is afforded to the believer in the death and resurrection of our Lord. The sinner believes in what was done at the Cross and is justified. The believer believes in what was done at the Cross and is sanctified. It is all through the Spirit.

There are some of you reading these words who are bound by sin of some sort, and yet, you love the Lord with all of your heart. The reason you are dominated by the sin nature is because you don't have the help of the Holy Spirit. That means that even though the Holy Spirit is most definitely present within you, still, you are trying to overcome this thing, what-ever it might be, within yourself, and the Holy Spirit will not function in that capacity.

You must turn your faith to the Cross and understand that Jesus defeated every power of darkness there and, as well, broke every grip of sin. That means He broke the grip of sin from you. You are to understand that it happened at the Cross, and your faith in Christ and the Cross guarantees the help of the Holy Spirit, which will then give you victory for which you have so long sought.

UNDERSTANDING THE CROSS OF CHRIST

Let's say for the sake of argument that you as a believer understand Christ and the Cross and have embraced it fully, but yet, you seem to still be struggling with some sin, whatever it might be. The thoughts have entered your mind that maybe this thing doesn't work. Without me going into a lot of detail, please understand that the Cross always works. It's you and me who do not work.

Then there is something else to consider: Even though your faith is in Christ and the Cross exactly as it ought to be, the Lord will still allow Satan certain latitude within your heart and life. He does it to test your faith. In fact, every single thing the Lord does with us is a test of faith. How will we act? How will we react?

Now, here's something else you must learn and understand: When you fail—I didn't say *if* you fail, but *when* you fail (in fact, you will fail many times)—but if you don't quit, the Lord will not quit, and you will eventually come out victorious.

As a child of God, you will lose many battles, but if you don't quit, you haven't lost the war. In fact, you are guaranteed to win the war if you do not quit, give up on the Lord, and once again begin to put faith in yourself, which is the sure road to disaster.

I don't want you to think that once your faith is in Christ and the Cross, as it ought to be, that everything is then the proverbial bed of roses—that Satan won't tempt you anymore, and there will never be another problem. That's not the way it is. I wish I could say that as a child of God with your faith in the right object, you will never fail again, but that's not true. You will. You should not, you ought not, and you don't have to, but, knowing the flesh, you will fail, regrettably, many times. However, the day will come when you will have total victory within your heart and within your life, and sin will not dominate you anymore. No, that doesn't mean sinless perfection, but it does mean that you will not be dominated by sin that has caused you all types of problems in the past.

THE HOPE OF RIGHTEOUSNESS

The phrase, *"wait for the hope of righteousness,"* refers to the full realization of righteousness that cannot come about until the resurrection. Paul also put it this way, *"The hope which is laid up for you in (the) heaven(s)"* (Col. 1:5). He also said, *"Looking for that blessed hope"* (Titus 2:13).

This does not mean that the believer does not have righteousness presently, for we certainly do. In fact, we have the perfect, pure, spotless righteousness of God, which is afforded by faith, and we have it in totality. We just don't have all the rewards or results yet of this righteousness.

The atonement provided for all things lost in the fall; however, the full fruit of the atonement has not yet been realized. That's the reason that Paul also said, *"Ourselves also, which have the firstfruits of the Spirit, even we ourselves groan within ourselves, waiting for the adoption, to wit, the redemption of our body"* (Rom. 8:23).

WHAT IS RIGHTEOUSNESS?

Righteousness is that which is right. It is the perfection of God, in other words, perfect morality. It is simplified in the Ten Commandments but involves far more than that.

With God's standard being perfection, it cannot be attained by man, at least within himself. Yet man keeps trying, and that's why the great animosity is in man's heart against Christ.

Due to the fall, man has a built-in depravity, a propensity toward evil; in effect, a hatred of God, whether he realizes it or not. This is because in the garden, man grasped at equality with God by robbery. In other words, Adam by robbery sought to exalt himself to the dishonoring of God. The last Adam— the Lord Jesus Christ—humbled Himself to the honoring of God. The first Adam exalted himself and was humbled. The last Adam humbled Himself and was exalted.

Irrespective, due to the evil nature in man, there is an animosity toward God, and especially toward Christ, who alone can save man. So man attempts to devise his own righteousness, which God will never accept, and which angers man greatly (Rom. 1:18).

THE ANGER EXPRESSED

Such anger in the heart of man is expressed against God's righteousness, who is Jesus Christ, by opposing both Christ and those who follow Him. So, the righteousness of man is greatly angered at the imputed righteousness of God.

It's the philosophy and spirit of the world that says, "I did it my way," or "I'm all right, and you are all right." Such an attitude is awful in the world but is even worse in the church.

When man adds religious activity to his own definition of righteousness, his anger is then greatly exacerbated. In other words, the greatest persecution of the true righteousness of God, which centers up against the true followers of Christ, always comes from within the church. It is because of this double death of so-called worldly righteousness and religious righteousness. It was the cause of the first murder, with Cain killing his brother Abel. Abel offered up a lamb of the flock, which spoke of an innocent victim, hence, the sacrifice of the coming Christ. This is what God demanded and what Abel did, recognizing himself as a sinner in need of a redeemer and accepting God's way of redemption.

Conversely, Cain, in essence, said, "I'm not a sinner; I don't need a saviour, and I will offer up as sacrifice whatever I desire, which is the fruit of my hands." Consequently, God would not accept it, even as God cannot accept such efforts. It resulted in murder, and religious righteousness has been murdering imputed righteousness ever since.

TYPES OF RIGHTEOUSNESS

In view of the great significance of this subject, please allow us to look at the types of righteousness outlined in the Bible. Of course, only one particular kind of righteousness is acceptable to God, which is the righteousness of God. But let's look at this that man attempts to carry forth, and that which God gives freely upon faith:

- Relative righteousness. This is found in the great parable given by Jesus concerning the Pharisee and the publican. Jesus said, *"Two men went up into the temple to pray; the one a Pharisee, and the other a publican. The Pharisee stood and prayed thus with himself, God, I thank You, that I am not as other men are, extortioners, unjust, adulterers, or even as this publican"* (Lk. 18:10-11).

This is relative righteousness, which compares itself with others. The world is fond of doing this and the church as well. The person looks at another and imagines himself to be better because of some bad things he hasn't done or good things he has done. Never mind that all have spiritual leprosy, which presents one who has 100 sores on his body thinking he is better than the other who has 110 sores. It should be obvious that such is a righteousness that God cannot accept, but yet, untold millions are depending on this for salvation.

- Works righteousness. The same Pharisee said, *"I fast twice in the week, I give tithes of all that I possess"* (Lk. 18:12). So this Pharisee is attempting to make himself righteous by fasting twice a week and by giving money. He doesn't seem to realize that man's depraved spiritual condition cannot be alleviated by starvation or by giving money. But yet, the world and most of the church somehow think they can. It shouldn't be difficult to understand, but somehow it is.

I'll ask this question: If a person has AIDS, would fasting twice a week cure AIDS? Would giving money to the church or some charitable institution heal AIDS? Of course, we know these things will have no effect on that disease, plus a thousand and one other things we have not named. It's the same with man's spiritual condition. He tries to cure spiritual cancer with a spiritual aspirin tablet. It simply won't work! If man can see these things as it pertains to everyday life, why can't he see it as it pertains to his condition and to God? These things are not really hard to understand, yet man keeps going in the opposite direction of God. Actually, the reason is simple: Man is deceived. He doesn't really believe that he is as bad as he actually is, and neither is he as good as he thinks he is.

- Imputed righteousness. Imputed righteouness means that the righteousness of God will be given to anyone who will only ask for it and evidence faith in it. God's righteousness is spotless and pure, and Jesus paid a great price for it, actually, by the shedding of His blood at Calvary's Cross.

This righteousness He will give to anyone—any sinner—no matter how evil or bad he might be, if he will only ask and believe. It cannot be earned. It cannot be purchased. In fact, it is a righteousness that has absolutely nothing to do with man, did not originate with man, and has no place in man—it's all of God. It is freely given by Jesus Christ to anyone who will believe (Jn. 3:16; Eph. 2:8-9; Rev. 22:17). This is the righteousness of which Paul speaks and the righteousness which alone God will recognize. This righteousness guarantees eternal life and is given freely by Jesus Christ upon faith. It is a pure, perfect, and spotless righteousness. It is given by faith, which guarantees our justification, and it is kept by faith, which guarantees our sanctification.

BY FAITH

The short phrase, *"by faith,"* refers to the only manner in which the things of God can be received by man.

This means simply that the person is to believe that Jesus Christ is the Son of God, died on Calvary, in effect, becoming our substitute, and rose from the dead. The person must believe that Jesus did all of this for him, even though he is a lost sinner. When he believes this and acts upon it by accepting Christ as his Saviour, the Holy Spirit then goes to work and makes all of this an accomplished fact. Also, after being saved, the believer must continue to have faith on a daily basis that this great sacrifice of Christ on Calvary not only effected his salvation but, as well, made it possible for him to live a victorious life in Christ. In other words, it is his sanctification. Once again, faith in that guarantees the help of the Holy Spirit, which guarantees victory in every aspect of his daily living.

It is not only a matter of having faith. Most people, if not all, have faith in something, but what and in whom is faith that registered? In other words, what is the object of our faith?

It must be registered completely in Jesus Christ and Him crucified (I Cor. 1:23) in order for one to be saved and to be victorious.

In the last 40 years, the church has been taught much about faith. Some small amount of it very good; however, most, I think, has not been good because it is faith in something other than the Cross.

In other words, if one notices carefully the tenor of the Word of God, one will find that the faith demanded is faith in Christ and the Cross. Everything must come through the Cross, as everything can only come through the Cross.

Instead, too many have been taught to have faith in themselves, faith in their confession, faith in particular Scriptures (oftentimes pulled out of context), etc. All of that is superficial.

The faith must be in the Cross, that is, if God is to recognize it, even as the Holy Spirit through Paul related to us (Gal. 6:14).

THEOLOGICAL AND NOT CEREMONIAL

"For in Jesus Christ neither circumcision avails anything, nor uncircumcision; but faith which works by love" (Gal. 5:6).

As hard as Paul has been on circumcision and as much as it would serve his purpose to downgrade it in preference to uncircumcision, he nevertheless acknowledges that neither circumcision nor uncircumcision within themselves count for anything. This is further evidence that his concern is theological and not ceremonial. It is a similar point to that made about eating meat offered to idols (I Cor. 8:8).

The second point is that true faith, having an ethical side, works itself out through love. This is what matters—this kind of faith! True, we are saved through faith rather than by works, but faith is no mere intellectual conviction as if a Christian could do as he wishes so long as he believes properly.

This is a ridiculous idea, as Paul writes elsewhere (Rom. 6:1-2). To believe is to place one's personal confidence in Christ, who loves us and gave Himself for us. Therefore, since Christians have learned love in such measure and at such a source, faith must issue in a genuine and self-denying love for others. In other words, if we really have true faith, we will have love for others.

A RELATIONSHIP WITH GOD

It is worth noting that Paul has come very close in this verse to giving a full and extremely beautiful definition of true salvation. "In this is the whole of Christianity," says Bingel. The sentence begins with a reference to those who are *"in Christ Jesus,"* so placing the emphasis both in point of order and in importance on God's act of engrafting a person into His Son.

It proceeds by repudiating the value of form or ceremony in determining a person's relationship with God. It ends with a unique emphasis upon the combination of faith and love to get toward both God and man. Paul does not combine the words in this manner anywhere else in his writings.

In Galatians 5:5-6, the three great terms—*faith, hope,* and *love*—appear together (I Cor., Chpt. 13; Col. 1:4-5; I Thess. 1:3).

IN JESUS CHRIST

The phrase, *"for in Jesus Christ neither circumcision avails anything, nor uncircumcision,"* refers to the fact that whether one is circumcised or uncircumcised—at least as it regards spiritual things— that has no power for anything in his life. In fact, that should be obvious. How can a cutting of the flesh on a baby, a boy, or a man effect anything spiritually? How could anyone think it could?

I'm certain that the Judaizers really appreciated these words by Paul, which, no doubt, endeared them to the apostle very readily. Of course, I say that in sarcasm. And yet, Christ was circumcised.

Christ in His circumcision undertook to perfectly obey all law, and in His baptism to fulfill all righteousness. He did it not in order to obtain merit for Himself, for He was sinless, but for those who should believe upon Him, and to whom all His moral perfection, ceremonial observance, and law-obedience are reckoned.

Salvation by works requires a perfect obedience. Such an obedience is impossible to imperfect man, hence, the hopelessness of salvation by works. The natural mind loves outward ceremonies, so Satan ministers to that desire by imposing on the sacrificial work of Christ a superstructure of outward sacraments and religious ceremonies and prayers and fastings, controlled by man-made priests. Thus, the confused human heart seeks to secure moral perfection but, in effect, destroys the gospel because it is not of faith but rather by works.

Faith is the medium of justification, and love is the evidence of justification. It fulfills the law—it is operative. However, as we shall see, a little legalism corrupts the whole gospel, and such is Satan's aim.

DOESN'T AVAIL ANYTHING

Man is not saved because he is circumcised, and neither is he condemned because he is not. The design of Christianity is to abolish these rites and ceremonies and to introduce a way of salvation that shall be applicable to all mankind alike.

As well, we should understand the statement given by Paul that if one is "in Christ," that one cannot be "in" something else at the same time, at least as it refers to one's salvation. In other words, people are fond of saying, "I'm *in* the church."

There is nothing wrong with that if, in fact, they are merely associating with other believers. However, if they think in some manner that being in that church constitutes some part of their salvation, they have just taken themselves out of Christ, that is, if they ever were in Christ.

Paul's opponents insisted that circumcision was essential to converts because it alone made one an heir of Abraham. In the foregoing argument, this has been decisively disproved.

ADDING WORKS TO FAITH

As well, Paul's statement about circumcision or uncircumcision does not mean that it made no difference if a believer was circumcised, thus adding works to his faith. Such would repudiate his faith, even as the apostle has already stated. Rather, it meant that this Jewish rite had no value for bringing a man to Christ or keeping a man in Christ. What it represented under the old covenant has now been fulfilled in Christ and, thereby, must be laid aside as worthless at this time.

As it regards salvation, being uncircumcised has no value either. Such distinctions are lost in Christ. The true values in God's sight are not material, physical, racial, or social—they're spiritual (I Cor. 13:13; II Cor. 4:18).

In fact, this was revolutionary. Many, even in the early Christian church, were unconvinced and even afraid of this position, even as we are now studying.

The idea is that no real spiritual power resides either in the observance of such ceremonies or in their abstinence. The same can be said for all other types of religious activities on which man may rely.

Another case in point in modern times is the prayer shawl. Some are taught that this will aid a person's prayers to a greater extent, and that the Lord will answer more readily. Actually, such has the very opposite effect. The simple reason is that those who rely on such are putting their faith in these things instead of Christ and the Cross. In fact, one could say the same identical thing about prayer shawls as Paul did here about circumcision.

FAITH AND LOVE

The phrase, *"but faith which works by love,"* is probably the most inclusive and extensive single statement on the nature of New Testament salvation that Paul ever made. While salvation is definitely by faith alone, the evidence that it is true faith that one actually possesses is the fact of love, which emanates from such faith. True faith expresses itself in love and is done through the power of the Holy Spirit.

In fact, Paul had already said some years before, *"Though I speak with the tongues of men and of angels, and have not charity* (love), *I am become as sounding brass, or a tinkling cymbal"* (I Cor. 13:1).

If our faith in Christ does not produce the love of God within us, that's a sure sign that whatever faith we are proclaiming is not the type of faith that places one in Christ.

Faith makes a man seek to do the will of Christ; love tells him what that will is. It is clear that the faith thus described by Paul does not stop short in a mere head notion, and so it is the same type of faith that is taught by James (James 2:14-26). All of this is produced by the Holy Spirit.

Faith in the Cross automatically centers up on the love of God, for Calvary was the greatest act of love that humanity has ever known and ever will know. So, if the believer anchors his faith in the Cross, the outcome cannot be anything but love as well as victory. Otherwise, it produces a stern self-righteousness, which is the bane of true Christianity and is the opposite of love.

ATHLETIC IMAGERY

"You did run well; who did hinder you that you should not obey the truth?" (Gal. 5:7).

In the first half of this section, the contrast has been between those who desire to add circumcision to Christianity and true believers who trust Christ alone. Paul has indicated the contrast by the pronouns *you* and *we*. Now the contrast changes to that between the false teacher (or teachers) designated as "the one who is throwing you into confusion," and "I, that is, Paul, who is teaching correctly."

Paul was fond of using athletic imagery to describe the Christian life. To him life was a race, demanding adherence to rules and discipline if the race was to be completed successfully and a prize obtained. Quite often he thought of himself as the competitor (I Cor. 9:24-27; Gal. 2:2; Phil. 3:13-14; II Tim. 4:7). At other times, as here, he applied it to the life of his converts.

The Galatians had begun the race well, Paul testifies. Theirs had not been merely an intellectual assent to certain truths, that is, mere orthodoxy divorced from Christian life and character. Neither was theirs the life of Christianity without doctrine. This is the full meaning of the phrase, *"obey the truth."*

Theirs was both a head and a heart salvation. Despite this good beginning, however, something had obviously gone wrong. Someone had hindered them.

Gaebelein said, "The Greek verb, 'enkopdo,' used here—a military term— refers primarily to setting up an obstacle or breaking up a road. In this context it probably refers to the illegal interference of a runner who cuts in ahead of another and, thereby, disadvantages him. Thus, so it seemed, the situation at Galatia was one in which the Galatians had already ceased in some measure to obey the plain truth of the gospel."

A GOOD BEGINNING

The phrase, *"you did run well,"* refers to a past tense action. Under the ministry of the apostle Paul, the Galatians had begun well and were making excellent progress in their spiritual growth.

The Holy Spirit through the apostle here likens the Christian life to a race. Nothing must be allowed to hinder our progress. We must be able to run well! Paul notes that these Galatians had once been so full of joy and of love in their faith, but now in an incipient relinquishment of their hope in Christ, it had left them cheerless. In consequence, they were ready to look abroad in quest of other grounds of assured confidence. Something had marred their once happy state.

The form of Christian life that the Galatian churches had in those days presented to view was apparently similar to that which, in an earlier day, Paul had described as marking the Thessalonian church (I Thess. 1:3), and at a later time, applauded the Colossians (Col. 1:4-6, 8).

The truth is, whenever faith is traded for works, the joy instantly dies. The reason is simple. If one attempts to earn salvation by works, how many works are enough? Or maybe the works aren't quite right. Such presents an endless quest that never slackens or slows but only increases. It is somewhat like walking or running on a treadmill. The motion is there, sometimes even extensively so, but the person is not going anywhere.

Many Christians are on a works treadmill. Because of the great activity, the frenzied pace, and the flowing perspiration, one is made to believe that he really is accomplishing something when, in reality, he is accomplishing nothing.

THE FAITH LIFE

By contrast, the faith life is not in doing but in trusting that which is already done. It is a beautiful life! A wonderful life! When one begins to live totally by faith in Christ and, more particularly, faith in what He did at Calvary, then one begins to understand what Jesus was talking about when He said, *"The thief* (the Devil) *comes not, but for to steal, and to kill, and to destroy: I am come that they might have life, and that they might have it more abundantly"* (Jn. 10:10).

But yet, and I think I exaggerate not, most of the church world gravitates toward the works religion, and for the simple reason that its great activity lends the impression that great things are going on when, in reality, nothing is going on.

If any believer will read this book, believe what he reads, and ask the Lord to give him revelation knowledge as he studies its contents, he can have victory in his life in a way that he has never known before. I know that these great truths that were given by the apostle Paul, which the Lord has helped us, I think, to open up to the reader, will help him to gain the victory that he seeks. In the first place, he can have victory over every single sin or habit that is so displeasing to the Lord. With this victory will also come a *"joy unspeakable and full of glory"* such as he has never known before (I Pet. 1:8). This will come so easily because the Holy Spirit is now performing the task.

FAILURE?

There is no need for any believer to suffer failure. There is no need for any believer to be overcome by sin. To be sure, I am speaking of every type of failure. This includes not only the sins of the flesh but, as well, pride, depression, fear, greed, and selfishness. In fact, the list is long. When Jesus died on Calvary and rose from the dead, He handled every single solitary problem by defeating all sin and demons, which came as a result of the fall. The victory is yours if you will only heed the Word of God and believe.

In fact, the Holy Spirit, I think, has helped us to make this so easy to understand that it's almost impossible not to believe. It is such a shame for us not to have the full benefits of all that He has done for us, considering the terrible price paid by Christ at the Cross. Considering that He did all of this for you and me, to miss out on any of the benefits must not be allowed to happen. We want to run well, and by the power and help of the Holy Spirit, we can run well!

HINDRANCES

The question, *"Who did hinder you that you should not obey the truth?"* refers to hindering the person on his journey.

Furthermore, the pronoun *who* lets us know that it was false teachers. In seducing the Galatians into abandoning the faith walk for the works walk, they had deprived these people of the ministry of the Holy Spirit, which guaranteed failure.

The question Paul asked was rhetorical, not for information. The apostle knew well enough who had slowed up the Christian growth of the Galatians.

The question asked by the apostle could be translated, "Who has cut you off from the way of grace?" To cut someone off in an athletic event was always for personal advantage. So, these false teachers had an agenda in mind that most certainly would not benefit the Galatians, but rather themselves.

FALSE APOSTLES

Much of the writing done by the apostle Paul was done to correct error that had come into the church, in fact, brought by false teachers. It is obvious that this was a great problem then, and if it was a great problem then, to be sure, it is a great problem now.

Satan uses every scheme at his disposal to get people to listen to the wrong preacher. Regrettably, he will use so-called religious leaders oftentimes in this effort. In fact, that's his greatest source of help. To be sure, I do not mean to say that all religious leaders fall into this category, for they don't; however, many, if not most, do.

With some few exceptions, denominational leaders are promoting their particular denomination instead of the Lord.

As well, many pastors fall into the same category. Their agenda is other things. There are a few who fall into the category of desiring your spiritual welfare above all things. They truly want you to grow in grace and the knowledge of the Lord and are very happy regarding how this is brought about, irrespective of the instruments used by the Lord. However, that number is few and far between.

THE TRUTH

First of all, it was Paul who preached the truth, and the truth was the grace message, which, of course, flows from the Cross.

Truth is a very precious commodity, so precious, in fact, that it is more valuable than silver and gold, or anything else for that matter. Of course, we are speaking of the truth of the gospel. This should be the quest of the believer after seeking truth.

Of course, we know the Word of God is truth, but to rightly interpret the Word is the single most important thing there could ever be. These false teachers were claiming to preach and teach the Word exactly as Paul; however, they were not rightly dividing the Word of Truth, which is an extremely serious offense.

I hope the reader can understand that this subject, as important as it is, should not be understated. For these people to believe this error would most definitely result in the loss of a victorious walk before God and even possibly the loss of their souls. Please understand that it was that serious then, and it is that serious now.

OBEYING THE TRUTH

Due to the proliferation of television, radio, and the printed page, opportunity to preach the gospel is more abundant than ever before. However, the same opportunity exists for the presentation of false doctrine as well. So, you the reader are bombarded with great amounts of false doctrine and a small amount of the truth. Please believe me, the latter has always been in short supply.

What you hear and accept—that to which you habitually listen—is going to decide many things in your life. The true gospel will lead you home. A false message will strip you and rob you of your place in Christ. However, make no mistake about it, it will be done subtly and with great promises attached.

For instance, untold numbers of Christians at this point in time listen carefully to the siren song of the modern greed teachers. Whatever they say, money is the goal, and prosperity is the promise. The truth?

The only ones who are going to get rich are the preachers. Besides losing your money, you are going to help support that which is not of God, and at the same time, you will grow spiritually lean in your soul. To be frank, the shores are littered with wrecks of faith burnouts, who thought Jesus could be used as a glorified bellhop, but they found out they were the only ones being used. For many, it is too late. They've grown discouraged and quit and now face the promises of God with little more than cynicism. In the thinking of that world, it really doesn't matter, for there is always a fresh crop of gullibles to take their place.

PERSUASION

"This persuasion comes not of Him who calls you" (Gal. 5:8).

Then, what more is to be said regarding false teaching and false teachers? Much indeed! In three succinct statements, Paul traces the origin, results, and end of such doctrine.

What is the origin of this teaching? "Well," says Paul, somewhat understating the case, "its origins do not lie in the one who calls you." The one who called the Galatians is obviously God (Gal. 1:6), but Paul does not say clearly that the origin of the false teaching is with Satan, although that is the case. The point is simply that the doctrine of salvation by works is not of God, but rather proceeds from that which is hostile to God's grace.

The word *persuasion* in the Greek is *peismone* and means "to induce one by words to believe." He is definitely speaking of the Judaizers and refers to their teaching as leaven, as the next verse proclaims, which, in Scripture, always refers to evil. Here, it refers to false doctrine.

Their persuasion was that they were attempting to get the Galatians to obey the law of Moses and to intermingle the observance of certain Jewish rites with the belief of the Christian doctrines in order to be saved.

OF HIM WHO CALLED YOU

The phrase, *"comes not of Him who calls you,"* as stated, is speaking of God.

The idea is this: Paul is saying that God had called the Galatians to grace, which they had accepted. It had changed their lives by bringing them out of deep sin and breaking all of the bondages of darkness. However, now these false teachers had come along and told them that their message was of God also. So, we have here a contradiction. God could not be calling the Galatians to grace and law at the same time; however, it seems that the Galatians had not quite put two and two together. They were influenced greatly by whatever methods were used by the false teachers and were now ready to embrace this other teaching. How so like modern Christians. How could they be pulled away from grace by something that was so diametrically opposed to grace? How were they seduced? Better yet, what caused them to respond to such seduction?

SELF-WILL

Before false doctrine can take hold in the heart and life of a believer, there must be something to which it can be attached. Without fear of contradiction, I feel it always can be said that certain something is self-will.

There is an old adage in the world which asks, "Can an honest man be conned?" While we certainly know that an honest man can be lied to, and, in fact, he can act upon that lie, that's not what we are discussing here.

For a person to be conned, there must be some larceny somewhere in his heart. For a believer to accept false doctrine, there must be self-will somewhere to which the doctrine can attach.

If God's will alone is sought, even as Jesus set the example, there are no openings of self-will for false doctrine to enter. Unfortunately, there is some self-will in all of us.

When the Lord called these Galatians, which was done through the ministry of the apostle Paul—that was the greatest day of their lives. It brought them from darkness to light. But now, they were about to go back into the darkness, that is, if they failed to heed the admonitions of Paul.

———✶———

Great King of Kings, why do You stay?
Why do You tarry upon Your way?
Why lingers the expected day?
Your kingdom come.

Life in its fullness is with Thee
Life in its holy liberty;
From death and chains this world set free:
Your kingdom come.

Oh King of glory, King of peace,
Bid all these storms and tumults cease,
Bring in Your reign of righteousness:
Your kingdom come.

Peace, gentle peace is on its way,
And holy love this earth to sway;
Hasten, O Lord, that glorious day;
Your kingdom come.

Oh, bid Your blessed gospel go
Forth to each child of sin and woe,
That all Your wondrous grace may know:
Your kingdom come.

THE YOKE OF BONDAGE

CHAPTER 3

LEAVEN

LEAVEN

"A LITTLE LEAVEN LEAVENETH the whole lump" (Gal. 5:9).

Paul speaks here of the present results of such teaching. It spreads. It is permeating, insidious, and, therefore, dangerous. No doubt, Paul is quoting a proverb at this point, even as he also seems to be doing in I Corinthians 5:6, but there is no need to identify it as a specific saying of the Lord as some have done.

The point is merely this: like yeast, false teaching grows and affects everything it touches. Therefore, this alone would justify Paul's alarm at the state of affairs in the Galatian churches.

So far, as the evidence goes, the leaven of old always consisted of a piece of fermented dough that had been kept over from a former baking. The lump of dough thus preserved was either dissolved in water in the kneading trough before the flour was added, or it was hidden in the flour and kneaded along with it. The bread thus made was known as leavened.

Due to its fermentation, leaven implies a process of corruption. Consequently, the figurative uses of leaven in the New Testament reflect the ancient view of it as "corrupt and corrupting." With some few exceptions, it is always used in a bad sense, even as Paul now alludes to the subject.

FALSE DOCTRINE

Paul is referring to false doctrine as leaven and, in effect, states that there is a spirit behind false doctrine, which ultimately guarantees the corruption of the whole. If false doctrine is allowed to remain, it will ultimately overcome all true doctrine. A perfect example is the doctrine of unconditional eternal security, which is believed by many in the Baptist church.

This is false doctrine pure and simple, even as Paul addresses the subject in Galatians 5:4. As a result, this doctrine now permeates the entirety of the Baptist denomination, having overcome all the truth that was there. In other words, it leavens the whole lump.

Another example: the United Pentecostal people, who teach that one has to be baptized in water to be saved. As well, they teach that one must be baptized by a certain formula, and that one must also speak with other tongues. To be frank, this is little different than the Mosaic law encouraged by the Judaizers. Consequently, this error (leaven) pretty well now permeates the whole.

Another example is the Church of God (Lee University), whose leaders, some years ago, embraced humanistic psychology until at the present time, this is about all that is left. The leaven has insidiously spread. Regrettably, the Assemblies of God has followed suit.

GIVEN BY THE HOLY SPIRIT

We must understand that this statement concerning leaven as given by Paul is not just a little trite saying offered by the apostle. The Holy Spirit chose this word. He is telling us of the danger of false doctrine, and how a little mixture into that which is true will ultimately take over the truth until there is nothing left but the false. It is not possible to be otherwise.

As we have previously stated, when a rotten apple is placed in a barrel full of good apples, the good apples do not heal the bad apple, but the opposite is always the result. In other words, the bad apple, if allowed to stay, will ultimately corrupt the entire barrel. We are actually being told here that this is, in essence, a law and, consequently, will happen irrespective of good intentions. Consequently, we must guard our hearts. This is the reason that Jesus constantly said, *"He who has ears to hear, let him hear"* (Mat. 11:15).

CONFIDENCE

"I have confidence in you through the Lord, that you will be none otherwise minded: but he who troubles you shall bear his judgment, whosoever he be" (Gal. 5:10).

The nature of evil—to spread—does not necessarily mean that God will permit evil to ultimately triumph. In fact, its end, at least as far as the true body of Christ is concerned, is the very opposite. In completing his analysis of the situation, Paul, therefore, concludes with an optimistic expression of his confidence that the Galatians will return to a right mind. He believes that the false teacher (or false teachers), whomever he is or however important he may seem to be, will suffer God's judgment. Paul's use of the singular, "he who," must not be overstressed, for he could very well be speaking of several.

The phrase, *"I have confidence in you through the Lord,"* seems to imply that in seeking the Lord about this matter of the Galatians, the apostle had been informed by the Holy Spirit that they would heed the true message given. Paul had laid it out so carefully and so clearly that it was impossible not to see what he was saying, that is, if a person wanted to do right. In respect to what the Lord had given him to tell them, Paul had come to a settled persuasion or conviction regarding them. This teaching comprises the greatest teaching in the Word of God as it regards a rejection of the flesh and dependence on the Spirit.

THE REFUSAL OF WRONG DIRECTION

The phrase, *"That you will be none otherwise minded,"* tells us that Paul expected the Galatians to take no other view of the source of the Judaizers' message than he took, namely, that it did not come from God but from an evil source and that the leaven of the Judaizers was false doctrine.

Let's go back to the leaven of the previous verse. As stated, it operates on the principle of fermentation and is an apt symbol of moral and spiritual corruption. A very small lump readily permeates the entire bread dough. The Lord also uses it as a symbol of the false doctrines of the scribes and Pharisees (Mat. 16:6-12).

In this case, it referred to the insidious work of the Juda-izers, which was slowly permeating the spiritual life of the Galatian churches.

The idea is that Paul was more alarmed over its insidious nature than over the extent to which it had already permeated the churches.

Every believer should look at his own life as it is lived for the Lord in the same capacity. If not rooted out and for-saken, the slightest sin or fault will ultimately engulf the whole. That is the nature of sin, and, therefore, it cannot be contained. This means that it's not possible to come to terms with sin or failure in any manner. As stated, it must be rooted out, and that means taken out by the roots to where there is no trace left. The person must be all of God and none of the world.

In fact, this is at least one of the great office works of the Holy Spirit in the believer's life, which is to act as a check, a warning, or a fence, if you will (Jn. 16:13-15; I Pet. 2:9).

OTHERWISE MINDED

To be otherwise minded means to accept and embrace a doctrine that is not the truth. The two words—otherwise minded—are critical.

The major problem in the modern church is preachers who are afraid to take a stand because of what their peers will think. All too often preachers seek the applause of fellow preachers far more than they seek the will of God. They want to be accepted; consequently, they are loath to take a stand on something that will bring about controversy; therefore, the leaven of false doctrine gains a greater and greater hold.

I love my brothers in the Lord and certainly desire their approval and well-wishes; however, I do not care nearly as much about that as I do pleasing the Lord. Other preachers are not my source, and neither are they my superiors. That distinction belongs only to the Holy Spirit. He is the one who gives me leading, guidance, and direction. He is the one whom I seek to follow. If I please all men and fail Him, in reality, I have pleased no one at all.

A STAND

To take this stand, I have had to give up almost everything. Denominational leaders have plainly said that if that stance was followed, they would oppose us in every way possible. That means making every effort to keep our telecast off the air. It means doing everything possible to destroy our financial base. It means, as well, doing all within their power to destroy any confidence the people might have in us. Nevertheless, I am very thankful to the Lord that I can say that I preach the same gospel today as I did yesterday. Thanks to the Lord, I know a little bit more about what I preach, and by the grace of God, I have grown in the Lord. Correspondingly, He has given me greater truths, but the basic foundation of the message has not changed.

In fact, one Secret Service agent based in Washington, D.C., a man, incidentally, whom I did not know, told one of my associates, "Well, this one thing I can say, Jimmy Swaggart preaches the same message now as he always did."

Coming from a man who does not profess salvation, I consider that a compliment.

THE MESSAGE

I have not had to change for the simple reason that the message I have always preached is the right message and does not need to change. It has brought untold thousands of souls to a saving knowledge of Jesus Christ and brought thousands of believers to a baptism with the Holy Spirit. It has seen untold numbers delivered from every type of bondage known to hell itself. It was right then, and it is right now.

I do not enjoy at all the opposition by much of the church world that has been manifested against my person and my ministry. I wish it was not that way; however, that is not my primary concern, but rather pleasing the Lord.

I realize that, due to the propaganda of religious leaders, most Christians think that such opposition is because of other things; however, that is patently untrue. It is because of the message that I preach and the anointing of the Holy Spirit upon that message.

The reader must understand that the salvation of souls, believers being baptized with the Holy Spirit, sick bodies being healed, and people being delivered by the power of God are not the first concerns of most preachers. Neither is the name of the Lord being glorified a priority with most preachers.

In truth, the well-wishes and accolades of other preachers is the first concern of most ministers; therefore, they compromise the message, that is, if they have truly had any convictions to begin with. Incidentally, these things of God can only come about as a result of right doctrine being preached.

JUDGMENT ON FALSE APOSTLES

The phrase, *"But he who troubles you shall bear his judgment, whosoever he be,"* tells us several very important things.

The apostle predicted here the judgment that will ultimately strike down false teachers, and at the same time, he expressed the confidence that he had in the Lord that the Galatians would stand fast in the truth.

It is so human to notice the apostle's uneasiness when he thought of them as feeble men, and his confidence when he thought of them as in the Lord. Greater was his agitation here than in Corinth. Moral questions grieved him there, but here the foundations of the gospel were in question, and the glories attaching to the person and work of Christ were supremely precious to the apostle's heart.

The word *troubles* in the Greek is tarasso and means, as it is here used, "the act of disturbing the faith of someone."

The word *bear* in the Greek is bastazo and here speaks of "a grievous burden." The judgment of God would be the grievous burden that anyone would have to bear who would disturb the faith of the Galatian Christians, or anyone else for that matter.

WHOSOEVER HE BE

The phrase, *"whosoever he be,"* could indicate either:

- That Paul did not know personally these adversaries
- That judgment would be theirs regardless of who they were

This is a sobering thought, and as the reader should understand, it is given by the Holy Spirit. This is not merely something Paul is saying but is actually a decree from the Lord.

In fact, the judgment of which Paul speaks is not to be ladled out by Paul, or any other man for that matter, but rather by the Lord. Irrespective of whom the believer may be, God does not give him the right to punish other believers. Ever how wrong the person might be, and even if fellowship has to be withdrawn, judgment belongs strictly to the Lord and to no one else (Rom. 12:19).

I speak this in the capacity of denominational leaders, and others for that matter, who attempt to destroy the ministry of those with whom they do not agree. This is grossly unscriptural and will always ultimately garner the judgment of God. It is one thing to withdraw fellowship, but it is something else altogether to engage in judgmental destruction against a fellow believer. As well, fellowship should not be withdrawn except for two reasons:

1. If false doctrine is being preached, such as that espoused by the Jews and Judaizers, then fellowship has to be withdrawn. By false doctrine, I do not speak of peripheral beliefs, but rather the core belief of salvation. The

Judaizers were advocating law as the thruway of salvation, which was actually a repudiation of Christ and the atonement. Consequently, there could be no fellowship. Many preachers differ in interpretation as it regards certain particulars in the Word of God, such as prophecy, etc. However, that poses no ground for disfellowship.

2. An open moral rebellion and refusal to repent is the other ground for disfellowship. An example is given in I Corinthians, Chapter 5. However, if repentance is engaged, fellowship must be continued, even as Paul outlines in II Corinthians, Chapter 2.

THE OFFENSE OF THE CROSS

"And I, brethren, if I yet preach circumcision, why do I yet suffer persecution? then is the offence of the Cross ceased" (Gal. 5:11).

What does Paul mean by saying, *"If I yet preach* (am still preaching) *circumcision"*?

The most likely explanation is simply that Paul's words are a reply to an accusation that he did preach circumcision when it suited him, however unfounded or unlikely that accusation was. The accusation could have originated from views such as those expressed in I Corinthians 7:18 or from the fact that Paul had once encouraged Timothy to be circumcised, which is more likely the case (Acts 16:1-3).

The *"offence of the Cross"* is an important concept to Paul and is a highly important reference in this context. The Greek word means a "trap, snare, or temptation." Paul uses it in the sense of that which is so offensive to the natural mind that it arouses fierce opposition, but why should Paul link his refusal to approve circumcision for Gentiles to the offense of the Cross?

Obviously, it's for the same reason that he opposed circumcision or any other work of the flesh generally. All of these things—feasts, circumcision, legal observances, or anything symbolizing external religion today—are of man and part of a system that seeks to obtain standing before God through merit, which cannot be done.

In opposition to this, the Cross proclaims man's complete ruin in sin to the degree that nothing he does or can do can save him and, thus, also proclaims man's radical need for God's grace, which can only come through the Cross.

The natural man does not understand such teaching (I Cor. 2:14) and, in fact, hates it because it strips away any pretense of spiritual achievement. It is only by the gift of God's Spirit, but that which was once a trap to him becomes his greatest boast and glory (Gal. 6:14).

FALSE DOCTRINE

The phrase, *"And I, brethren, if I yet preach circumcision,"* no doubt, proclaims the fact that these false teachers had claimed that Paul preached circumcision, as well, and, as stated, were probably referring to Timothy.

The apostle encouraged Timothy to be circumcised because he was a Jew and was joining Paul's evangelistic party. Inasmuch as Paul was attempting to reach the Jews as well as Gentiles, he knew that if this was not done, his detractors would make much of the fact and cause him problems. However, Paul insisting upon this as it regarded Timothy in no way did so as it referred to one's salvation. It was only as a matter of expediency in attempting to reach the Jews for Christ.

Paul had never enjoined circumcision as necessary to salvation. He, as well, had never complied with Jewish customs where there was any danger that it would be understood that he regarded them as at all indispensable, or as furnishing a ground of acceptance with God.

WHAT DO WE PREACH?

The idea of this phrase goes beyond the accusation leveled against Paul, but rather strikes at the very heart of what we preach as ministers of the gospel. In fact, what do we preach? Better yet, what *should* we preach?

As it regards the people who sit under a particular ministry, what is preached is what they are going to receive and, consequently, what they will be.

Circumcision was being preached by the Judaizers; consequently, their trust would be in law and not grace. If our primary message is prosperity, the people are going to center up on that, even as they are presently doing. If ethics are preached as a way of salvation, then the people who listen to that message, as false as it might be, will believe that which they hear. So, what we preach and what you hear is the single most important thing in the world as it regards one's salvation, and there is nothing more important than that.

The truth is, if the Galatians, or anyone else for that matter, had heeded these Judaizers, which they were on the border of doing, they would bring upon themselves tremendous trouble and possibly even the loss of their souls. Consequently, I think one can see how so very important all of this actually is. That's the reason Paul so strongly opposed this particular type of preaching— he knew what the results would be.

What is the true message that is to be preached by all ministers of the gospel? Paul tells us in the next phrase.

PERSECUTION

The conclusion of the question, *"Why do I yet suffer persecution?"* tells us something very important.

Any message other than the Cross draws little opposition. In Paul's case, the book of Acts records the fact that he was continually being persecuted by the Jews because of his break with the Mosaic economy. It was as a Pharisee that he had once preached circumcision. After coming to Christ, this ceased. Paul's contention was, and rightly so, that if he was still preaching circumcision as the legalizers claimed, why were the Jews persecuting him even to the point of trying to take his life?

However, this particular subject ranges much further than the persecution leveled by the Jews against Paul. It involves itself in the entirety of the presentation of the gospel.

THE DOCTRINE OF THE ATONEMENT

The doctrine of the atonement (the Cross) is offensive to the self-righteous mind, for it declares that man is morally lost, wicked and hopeless, helpless and dead—at least to spiritual things—and that he can only be recovered by being re-created.

This re-creation takes place when he believes upon Christ as the atoning Saviour. This means that man cannot be rehabilitated as the world of psychology claims. As well, he cannot be reformed. So, it is not rehabilitation or reformation that is needed, but rather re-creation.

Man denies that he is altogether lost, and he claims that he can add something to the sacrifice that Christ infinitely accomplished for him at Calvary. However, such an addition destroys the gospel, for it denies the infinite perfection of Christ's sacrifice. If that sacrifice was infinite, then there is no room for human additions to it in order to add to its perfection.

To preach Christ and good works—proudly named the "ethical gospel" — does not involve persecution, but to preach the true gospel, which involves the Cross, definitely does involve persecution.

THE OFFENSE OF THE CROSS

The phrase, *"Then is the offence of the Cross ceased,"* refers to the fact that if Paul, or any other preacher for that matter, will cease to preach the Cross as the only way of salvation, and the only way of sanctification, then opposition and persecution will cease.

What made the Cross an offense to the Jew? Paul tells us in the words, *"If I yet preach circumcision … Then is the offence of the Cross ceased."* That is, if circumcision was preached as one of the requirements of salvation, then the Cross of Christ would cease to be an offense. Thus, the offensiveness of the Cross to the Jew lay in the teaching that believers in the Lord Jesus are free from Mosaic law.

This was the very point and issue when the Sanhedrin was trying Stephen. The charge was not that he was worshipping the crucified one; it was that he was speaking blasphemous words against the Jewish temple and the law of Moses (Acts 6:13-14).

Chrysostom, commenting on this same thing, said, "For even the Cross, which was a stumblingblock to the Jews, was not so much so as the failure to require obedience to ancestral laws. For when they attacked Stephen, they said not that he was worshipping the Crucified, but that he was speaking against the law and the Holy Place."

In fact, before coming to Christ, Saul persecuted the church for the same reason (Acts 9:1-2; Gal. 1:13-14).

The Cross was offensive to the Jew because it set aside the entire Mosaic economy. It offered salvation by grace through faith alone without the added factor of works performed by the sinner in an effort to merit the salvation offered. All of this goes to show that the Jew of the first century had an erroneous concept of the law of Moses, for that system never taught that a sinner was accepted by God on the basis of good works. The idea is this: Take away the Cross and omit the atoning death of Christ, and all difficulty is gone—but so is all salvation gone as well.

THE PRESENT OFFENSE

As the Cross was an offense then, the Cross is an offense now. Even though the Jews are not a factor presently as they were in the days of Paul, others have taken their place.

In fact, as we have already alluded, many churches presently don't proclaim the Cross at all, or they only pay it lip service, rather proclaiming an ethical gospel. This refers to man alleviating his spiritual condition, in other words, making himself right with God by the performing of good works or abstaining from bad things. His salvation is based upon his ethics, which denies the Cross of Christ.

Others proclaim the necessity of water baptism, the Lord's Supper, or tongues as being necessary for salvation. While these things are important, they have nothing to do with salvation, and when we lift them up and, thereby, place our faith in them, we are, in effect, repudiating the Cross.

Many years ago, the denominational churches forsook the Cross in favor of humanistic psychology as it regarded the cure for the sinful aberrations of man. Regrettably, beginning sometime in the 1960s, most of the Pentecostal denominations began to follow suit. This is a far greater sin than appears on the surface.

It amounts to a wholesale departure from the Cross in favor of the wisdom of man, which James said is *"earthly, sensual, devilish"* (James 3:15).

For the most part, the charismatic community has forsaken the Cross—that is, if they ever centered upon its veracity—in favor of faith, but it's faith in the wrong object. The faith that they promote, of which we speak, is little directed toward the Cross, if at all, but rather toward self. Of course, there are exceptions in all of these particular directions, but not many.

As we have repeatedly said, there has been very little preaching of the Cross in the last few decades. As a result, cleverly presented false doctrines have taken its place.

However, let it be known that there is no hope for man outside of the Cross of Christ.

WHAT DOES IT MEAN TO PREACH THE CROSS?

The *"preaching of the Cross"* (I Cor. 1:18) proclaims the vicarious, atoning sacrifice of Christ on the Cross of Calvary as the answer to all of the spiritual needs of man. It was there that Jesus paid the sin debt, which broke the grip of sin in the human race, at least for those who will believe (Jn. 3:16). It was there that the enmity that stood between God and man was removed, at least for those who believe. It is faith in the Cross and the Cross alone that guarantees salvation, and in every respect. This refers not only to the initial experience of being saved but one's everyday walk before God as well. In other words, everything comes through the Cross—salvation, the baptism with the Holy Spirit, divine healing, deliverance from all sin, the fruit of the Spirit, the gifts of the Spirit, and the victorious overcoming Christian life; in other words—everything. It is all through the Cross, which, in reality, is the very foundation of the new covenant. In fact, the Cross of Christ is the meaning of the new covenant, with Jesus being that new covenant.

In effect, the meaning of the new covenant was given to the apostle Paul (Gal., Chpt. 1).

That means that if sinful man, failing man, hurting man, or man in any capacity is directed toward anything other than the Cross of Christ, in effect, false doctrine is being presented. It is that naked, crude, shameful, painful, and hurting sacrifice offered by Christ at Calvary that is the only hope of lost mankind. There is no other. Nothing must be taken from the Cross, and nothing must be added to the Cross. We might very well say that the Cross of Christ alone stands between man and eternal hell.

THE CHURCH AND THE CROSS

So, when the greed message is held up, in other words, given preeminence, this is a denial of man's true problem—sin—and man's true solution—the Cross. Whenever humanistic psychology is recommended, this is a denial of what Jesus did at the Cross, and a denial that this one supreme sacrifice is the true answer for the problems of mankind.

In fact, whereas the Cross is only one way, error provides many ways, but all wrong.

This is where the church runs aground, in its failure to preach the Cross, to proclaim the Cross, and to hold up the Cross as the answer for hurting humanity. Any preacher preaching anything other than the Cross is not preaching the gospel. It is just that simple. As well, for any preacher who preaches the Cross, and thank God some few still do, persecution will come from every corner, but it will be mostly from the church for the simple reason that the doctrine of the atonement is offensive to the self-righteous mind. The Cross shows man how bad he really is, and how unable he is to save or even improve himself, which he doesn't like to hear, especially religious man.

However, irrespective, the answer to all of man's ills is the Cross, the Cross, *the Cross!*

THE JUDAIZERS

"I would they were even cut off which trouble you" (Gal. 5:12).

This remark by Paul is directed straight against the legalizers (Judaizers). If these false teachers insisted upon circumcision as a requirement of salvation, it is wished that they would not stop with circumcision in their zeal for ordinances, but rather would go on to castration. Castration in the realm of religious activity was known to citizens of the ancient world. It was frequently practiced by pagan priests as in the cults of Attis-Cybele, which was prominent in Asia, and with which the believers in Galatia would have been familiar.

For Paul to compare the ancient Jewish rite of circumcision to pagan practices even in this way is startling. For one thing, it puts the efforts of the Judaizers to have the Gentiles circumcised on the same level as abhorred pagan practices. For another, it links their desire for circumcision to that which even in Judaism disbarred one from the congregation of the Lord (Deut. 23:1).

To many in our day, Paul's expression might sound coarse, and his wish reprehensible. We may be sure that Paul did not speak in a malicious spirit or in ill temper. He spoke out of a concern for the gospel of grace and for God's truth.

In fact, it was the Holy Spirit who told him to say what he did, even down to the very words.

Stott says, "If we were as concerned for God's church and God's Word as Paul was, we too would wish that false teachers might cease from the land."

CUT OFF

The phrase, *"I would they were even cut off,"* no doubt, caused many in the church of Jerusalem to think somewhat harshly of Paul.

Unfortunately, the Jewish segment of the church, which was altogether in Judaea, was still trying to keep the law of Moses. This proved a constant source of irritation for Paul and a great hindrance to the work of God in general. This does not mean that James and the elders in that church approved of what these false teachers were doing and saying—not at all! However, by the simple fact that the old Mosaic customs were being continued in the church in Jerusalem, which included circumcision, it provided encouragement for these false teachers. As one can presently see from the Scriptures, the carrying on of the Mosaic economy after the crucifixion and resurrection of Christ, whether realized or not by its practitioners, was an insult to the finished work of Christ.

This word as given by Paul is somewhat of a throwaway statement. He is attempting to show the Galatians, and all others who would read this epistle for that matter, just how foolish and ridiculous such a practice actually was as it concerned salvation. Circumcision did not bring salvation and contributed nothing toward salvation even under the Mosaic law. So, how could it effect such presently, which these false teachers should have known? The fact is, not only did they not know anything about the salvation experience in Christ, but they really didn't even know anything about the Mosaic law either. If one objects to Paul's choice of words as it regards this statement, one must remember that it was the Holy Spirit who told him what to say, even down to these very words. Consequently, from this we should understand what the Lord thinks of false doctrine as well. The psalmist said, *"Through Your precepts I get understanding: therefore I hate every false way"* (Ps. 119:104).

TROUBLED BELIEVERS

In Galatians 5:12, the phrase, *"which trouble you,"* proclaims the tares that Satan had sown among the wheat. False doctrine has ever been a trouble to the church, and it is trouble to the church presently.

Recently at Family Worship Center, I preached on the Cross, actually, that which I have been doing quite heavily for the last several years. I am told that a young man was in the service from a neighboring town. He was invited by one of our men. After service, he said to the man who had invited him, "I have found me a church home. This is the first message on the Cross that I've heard in the last five years."

While I'm very pleased that he feels led of the Lord to come to Family Worship Center, at the same time, I am very sad that the preaching of the Cross has been neglected in the church or the churches that he had been previously attending. However, as I've said, in the last several decades, there has been very little preaching on the fundamental core of Christianity, which is the Cross of Jesus Christ. In fact, it has been all but ignored.

THE CROSS

On a personal basis, the Holy Spirit has taught me more about the Cross in the last 12 months than in all of my previous ministry put together. The truths He has opened up to me that I have attempted to put in this volume, as well as other volumes, have revolutionized my life, my ministry, and my thinking as it regards the gospel. I have always preached the Cross for salvation and have seen multiple tens of thousands brought to a saving knowledge of Jesus Christ, and I exaggerate not. However, before the Lord revealed the great truth to me concerning the Cross of Christ respecting our sanctification, I did not preach that great truth because I did not know anything about it. In fact, as it regards our sanctification—how we live for God on a daily basis, how we have victory over the world, the flesh, and the Devil, and how we grow in grace and the knowledge of the Lord—this great truth is not known presently in the Christian world except for those who have tuned to SonLife Broadcasting respecting our television network. Thank God, this network goes all over the world presently, and this truth is beginning to be known and understood, but only in the beginning stages. Please note the following, and I think it will help you to understand this that we believe Paul gave to us:

- Jesus Christ is the source of all things we receive from God (Jn. 1:1-3, 14, 29).
- The Cross of Christ is the means, and the only means, by which all of these great blessings are given to us (Rom. 6:3-14; I Cor. 1:17-18, 23; 2:2).
- With Jesus Christ being the source and the Cross being the means, Christ and the Cross must ever be the object of our faith. This is absolutely imperative (Gal. 6:14; Col. 2:10-15).
- With Christ as the source, the Cross as the means, and the Cross of Christ ever the object of our faith, then the Holy Spirit, who works entirely within the parameters of the finished work of Christ, will work grandly on our behalf, giving us victory over the world, the flesh, and the Devil (Rom. 8:1-11; Eph. 2:13-18).

SCRIPTURAL AND SPIRITUAL DECEPTION

The problem with error is that it is done in such a way that the intended victims are not aware of what is actually happening even though they are being troubled greatly. The truth is that the Galatians were on the way to changing their faith from the Cross to law, which, as Paul stated, would cause the loss of their souls if they continued in that direction. Consequently, there could be nothing more serious, more troublesome, or more awful than that. In fact, the entirety of the basis of Christianity lies in this great truth.

One's faith must be in the Cross, and the Cross totally, which means what Jesus did there in order to be saved. If anything is added to that, even as the apostle said about leaven, the Cross will little by little cease to be a focal point, with the error consuming all. That is the way of error if it's not rooted out.

So, Satan works diligently through his ministers (II Cor. 11:13-15) to shift the faith of the believer to other than that of the Cross. In fact, that is the one way that the believer can lose his soul. The reason is simple: If he ceases to believe in the Cross totally and completely as it regards salvation, but rather substitutes something else (even as religious as the something else may be), he has stepped outside of the foundation and basis of salvation. In other words, he has denied Christ, whether he realizes it or not. So, Satan wants the believer to put his faith in the church, in water baptism, in the Lord's Supper, in good works, or whatever—anything but Christ and the Cross.

THE SUBTILTY OF ALL OF THIS

Of course, Satan is very subtle in all that he does. Even if the Galatians had gone into law, they would not have thought in their minds that they had forsaken Christ. In their thinking, and according to what they had been told by these false teachers, they would have merely been adding something to

Christ that they had been told would make them holier and give them a deeper walk. So, in their thinking, Christ would not be forsaken; however, the truth is that in such a course, Christ would have been forsaken, whether they realized it or not. This is the terrible and horrible danger of false doctrine. It cloaks itself in religious phraseology, papers itself over with Scriptures, and is served up oftentimes as a "deeper walk," or a "deeper life." However, the truth is that Christ has been forsaken, so what happens now?

As stated, and as the Holy Spirit has pointed out through the apostle, the error, like leaven, will get larger and larger until it consumes everything that is believed by the individual. Then, the Cross, which is the true way of salvation and sanctification, will be pushed aside and finally ignored altogether.

In fact, that is the condition that much of the church is in presently. While it's not the law of Moses that's being promoted, it is the same thing in principle as it regards other particulars.

THE OLD RUGGED CROSS

I will give you an example: During a recent morning in service, we were singing the chorus of the old hymn, "The Old Rugged Cross." As most of you know, the words are as follows:

So I'll cherish the old rugged Cross,
Till my trophies at last I lay down,
I will cling to the old rugged Cross,
And exchange it someday for a crown.

One of the leading lights of the so-called faith ministry made a statement regarding singing songs about the Cross. In fact, he has made it any number of times. The words he said are to this effect: "No Christian should sing songs about the Cross. That's all in the past and holds no more significance for us presently. We are people of the resurrection and, therefore, new creations, and the Cross speaks of past miseries."

He then said, "If you try to cling to that old rugged cross, it's going to become more and more rugged."

Why would he say such a thing?

The fundamental teaching of the faith ministry is based on confession and not on the Cross. While it speaks of faith constantly, it is not faith in the Cross, not at all, but rather in oneself. While many would deny that, the truth is, it can be no other way.

They would claim that it's faith in the Word of God, but it's not. Even though Scriptures are used, they are used out of context. I say that because everything must be based on the Cross, and if not, it is heresy.

From Genesis 3:15, where the Cross in shadow is first mentioned, all the way through to Revelation 22:21, which speaks of the *"grace of our Lord Jesus Christ,"* the Bible proclaims the Cross as the centerpiece of all that is done.

In other words, it is the revelation of God. Grace stems totally and completely from the Cross—what Jesus there did—and in no other manner. So, irrespective of how much we may claim that our faith is in the Word of God, if we do not properly understand that the Word of God is in the Cross, and that the Cross is in the Word of God, then our direction is wrong.

JESUS ANSWERED THIS QUESTION HEAD ON

When Jesus asked His disciples, *"Whom do men say that I the Son of Man am?"* the answers were varied, with Jesus then saying, *"But whom do you say that I am?"*

Peter answered and said, *"You are the Christ, the Son of the living God."*

Jesus' answer was revealing. He said, *"Blessed are you, Simon Bar-jona: for flesh and blood have not revealed it unto you, but My Father who is in heaven"* (Mat. 16:13-17).

After giving further direction and promises, Jesus then began to reveal to them His soon coming death and resurrection. Of course, this spoke of the Cross, which was the very purpose of His coming.

The Scripture then says, *"Peter took Him, and began to rebuke Him, saying, Be it far from You, Lord: this shall not be unto You."*

Jesus then said to Peter, *"Get thee* (You get) *behind Me, Satan: you are an offense unto Me: for you savor not the things that be of God, but those that be of men."*

And then, *"If any man will come after Me, let him deny himself, and take up his cross, and follow Me"* (Mat. 16:22-24).

Jesus held up the Cross as the answer to the terrible problems of humanity, and anything that threatened that doctrine was concluded to be of Satan (Mat. 16:23). If that doesn't give us pause for thought, I don't know what will.

The preacher must preach the Cross; the church must proclaim the Cross; and the believer must live the Cross. In fact, that's the only way one can live.

The reasons are very simple: Everything comes through the Cross of Christ. So, don't let any preacher trouble you by espousing things that may look to be scriptural but, in fact, do not have the Cross as their foundation. Turn away from all such things, and do so immediately.

ONE MORE QUESTION MUST BE ASKED

Were these false teachers of Paul's day saved?

They emphatically were not! Their trust was in the law and not in the Cross, and until they came to the Cross, they could not be saved.

What about their modern counterparts?

As it regarded Paul's day, the case with these false teachers was clear-cut; however, many of the modern situations are not that clear-cut. Consequently, the judgment of each and every situation is up to the Lord unless it is obvious, as it is with some.

Many times preachers teach things simply because they've heard others teach the same thing. If it is right, that is well and good, but if not, problems begin to accrue. The point I am making is that oftentimes things are taught through ignorance. However, if the preacher is sincere, the Lord will ultimately open up the right way to him. If he refuses to walk in that right way, then he goes into heresy, etc.

The truth is, all of us are in a state of growth, and no one has all the light on any given subject. Even Paul said, *"Brethren, I count not myself to have apprehended"* (Phil. 3:13), the meaning of which is obvious. The Lord is merciful and gracious with us all, looking more so at the heart than anything else. Irrespective of whether false doctrine is taught out of ignorance or is the product of a settled course, even as the Judaizers of Paul's day, the damage will be the same.

In glory bright He'll come again,
Who in our stead endured the pain,
And was the Lamb for sinner's slain:
The Lord will come again.

Ye saints of God, for whom He died,
In faith and hope, and love abide,
As rocks unmoved 'mid swelling tide
Until He come.

Stand, soldier, stand; the battle's roar
In that great day shall sound no more;
Then face the foe, and ne'er give o'er,
Until He come.

Toil, workman, toil, your gracious Lord
Will give you soon a full reward:
Then toil, obedient to His Word,
Until He come.

Sing, pilgrim, sing, Christ's mighty hand
Will bring you safe to that bright land:
Then sing; it is thy Lord's command,
Until He come.

THE YOKE OF BONDAGE

CHAPTER 4

AN OCCASION TO THE FLESH

AN OCCASION TO THE FLESH

"FOR, BRETHREN, YOU HAVE been called unto liberty; only use not liberty for an occasion to the flesh, but by love serve one another" (Gal. 5:13).

FREEDOM

Paul has already spoken of freedom. From one point of view, Galatians is almost entirely about freedom. Still, up to this point, Paul has not yet defined it, at least not in practical terms dealing with the ethical life. Now he does so. He shows not only the true nature of Christian freedom, but also that it is only through the life of the Spirit and by the Spirit's power that the Christian can live for God and not fulfill the desires of his sinful nature. The Holy Spirit always works through the Cross of Jesus Christ according to the price there paid and our faith in that finished work. Negatively, freedom in Christ is not license. Positively, it is service both to God and to man. It expresses itself in the great Christian virtues. This latter point is emphasized by two contrasting catalogs of the works of the flesh versus the fruit of the Spirit.

FAITH THROUGH LOVE

One reason Paul adds this section to this letter is to show what he means by faith expressing itself through love. Another is apparently to counter developing strife and divisiveness in the churches of Galatia, for the verses speak of a biting, devouring, and destroying of each other that seems to have been taking place. However, the greatest reason is, undoubtedly, Paul's desire to complete his portrait of true Christianity by showing that the freedom we have been called to in Christ is a responsible freedom that leads to holiness of life.

Called to freedom? Yes, but this is a freedom to serve God and others as love dictates. That Paul would have had this point uppermost in mind is evident from the apparent and quite understandable fear within Judaism that a faith without law would not be sufficiently strong to resist the debauchery of paganism.

SINFUL SELF-INDULGENCE

Verse 13, like verse 1, is transitional and marks a new beginning. The fact that the pronoun *you* is emphasized in the Greek by being placed first in the sentence shows that Paul is building on the confidence expressed earlier as to what side the Galatians are on. The language of the verse shows that Paul is echoing the original challenge of verse 1: It is for freedom that Christ has set us free.

On the other hand, in the first instance, Paul followed his statement with a warning about falling again into slavery. In this case, the warning is changed into the demand not to allow this freedom to become an excuse for sinful self-indulgence. Here, the contrast is between indulgence and the serving of one another in love. Paul says that the Christian is not to allow this freedom—the freedom in Christ he has been writing about— to become a beachhead for the armies of indulgence to gain a foothold in his life.

When Paul speaks of *sarx* (flesh, sinful nature), he means all that man is and is capable of as a human being apart from the Holy Spirit in his life. In other words, anything in the spiritual sense that is birthed by man and not by the Holy Spirit, irrespective of one's consecration, can be said to not be of God. The Holy Spirit must birth all things spiritual within our hearts and lives, or it is unacceptable to God.

SLAVES OF ONE ANOTHER

It is ironic that, having urged the Galatians not to become slaves to law, Paul should now encourage them to become slaves of one another, for that is what the verb translated *"serve"* means. It is a paradox, but the paradox is instructive.

The Galatians are to be slaves of one another, though this slavery is not at all like the first. In fact (this is the paradox), it is the Christian form of being free.

Slavery to sin is involuntary and terrible. A man is born into sin (Ps. 51:5) and cannot escape it (Rom. 7:18). Slavery to law, which comes by choice, is foolish and burdensome. In fact, Peter said at the great council at Jerusalem, *"Now therefore why do you tempt God, to put a yoke* (the law) *upon the neck of the disciples* (followers of Christ)*, which neither our fathers nor we were able to bear?"* (Acts 15:10).

On the other hand, slavery to one another is voluntary and a source of deep joy. It is possible only because Christians are delivered through the presence and power of the Holy Spirit from the necessity of serving sin in their lives.

LIBERTY

The phrase, *"For, brethren, you have been called unto liberty,"* sums up the whole preceding argument, and looks ahead to what follows in that it introduces a whole new aspect of the matter of Christian liberty. I speak of the danger of abusing it.

There are those who have been accustomed to regarding law as the only controlling factor that stands in the way of self-indulgence and a free reign to sin. As well, there are those who have not been accustomed to a high standard of ethics. To those just mentioned, the teaching of Christian liberty might easily mean that there is nothing to stand in the way of the unrestrained indulgence of one's own impulses. In fact, during Paul's ministry, he often had his hearers react in this way to his teaching regarding grace. The questions in Romans 6:1 and 6:15, *"Shall we continue in sin, that grace may abound?"* and *"Shall we sin,*

because we are not under the law, but under grace?" were asked by
someone who did not understand grace.

Paul answers these questions in Romans, Chapter 6, by
showing that the control of the sinful nature over the individual is broken the moment he believes, and the divine nature is
imparted. Therefore, he hates sin and loves righteousness and
has both the desire and power through the Holy Spirit to keep
from sinning and to do God's will.

THE HOLY SPIRIT

In Galatians, Paul shows that the believer has come out from
under whatever control divine law had over him, and in salvation,
has been placed under a superior control. That is the indwelling
Holy Spirit, who exercises a stricter supervision over the believer
than law ever did over the unbeliever. His restraining power is
more effective than the law's restraining power ever was. He
gives the believer both the desire and power to refuse the wrong
and choose the right thing, which law was never able to do.

To have this help of the Holy Spirit, the believer, without fail, must place his or her faith exclusively in Christ and
the Cross, and maintain it even on a daily basis in Christ
and the Cross. What Jesus did at the Cross gives the Holy
Spirit the legal means to do all that He needs to do (Rom. 8:2).
It is imperative that the believer understand that the object
of our faith must ever be Christ and the Cross. If our faith is
in something other than Christ and the Cross, it is judged by
God as spiritual adultery. The Holy Spirit will not be a party

to such, as should be obvious. In other words, such a believer is being unfaithful to Christ.

Upon true faith (we continue to speak of the Cross), the believer, therefore, has passed out of one control into another. He has gone from the control of a mere system of legal enactments, which contains no power to help one carry out those enactments, into the control of a person—God the Holy Spirit.

When God abrogated the law at the Cross, He knew what He was doing. He did not leave the world without a restraining hand. That restraining hand is the Holy Spirit, but He is available only to believers.

We might quickly add that the Holy Spirit does not need the help of legalistic teachers in the church, who think they are helping Him control the church by imposing law on grace. Indeed, it is the general ignorance and lack of recognition of the ministry of the Holy Spirit that is responsible for the tendency in the church of adding law to grace. In fact, that is what this epistle to the Galatians is all about.

A RESTRAINT

There is a recognition of the fact that the flesh is still with the Christian, even though its power over him is broken and, consequently, a feeling that even the child of God needs a restraint put upon him. This is as it should be, but the mistake that is made so often is that the Mosaic law is substituted for the restraint of the Holy Spirit, and it is always with disastrous results. I know, for I have been there.

Not only does the law not restrain evil, but it brings out evil in the life of the believer because the fallen nature rebels against it (Rom. 7:7-13).

The Holy Spirit dealt with men before the Mosaic law was given. He still continues to do so; however, the difference in then and now is that He indwells the believer, which He did not do before Pentecost. As such, He has the cooperation, or at least is supposed to, of the Christian in His work of restraining evil. In fact, He will restrain evil in the church (the true church) until the church is taken to heaven in the resurrection—the rapture (II Thess. 2:7).

However, He will still be restraining evil during the great tribulation since He is omnipresent.

No preacher ever enables the Christian to whom he ministers to live a better Christian life by putting him under the Ten Commandments of Sinai. A policeman on the street corner is a far more efficient deterrent of lawbreaking than any number of city ordinances placed on posters throughout the city.

To acquaint the saint with the ministry of the indwelling Holy Spirit is far more productive for victory over sin than the imposition of the law, and we speak of law of any kind. The controlling ministry of the Holy Spirit is the secret of holy living, and that is what Paul is addressing here.

However, let us once again emphasize the fact that to have this restraining force and to have the power of the Spirit working within our hearts and lives, helping us to do what we cannot do within ourselves, always, and without fail, requires our faith to ever be in Christ and what He has done for us at the Cross

(Rom. 8:1-11). How the Holy Spirit works is little presently known to the modern church. To be sure, He works through the Cross and by the Cross. Of course, when we speak of the Cross, we aren't speaking of the wooden beam on which Jesus died, but rather what the Master accomplished at the Cross by the giving of Himself as a perfect sacrifice.

WHAT DID JESUS ACCOMPLISH AT THE CROSS?

First of all and foremost, He atoned for all sin—past, present, and future—and we speak of those who believe (Jn. 3:16). By atoning for all sin, He took away the right that Satan had to hold man captive. Sin gives the Evil One that right. The reason that the unredeemed are still in bondage is because they will not take advantage of what our Lord did at Calvary's Cross. It must be quickly said about believers, also, that if the believer places his faith in anything other than Christ and the Cross, this greatly hinders the Holy Spirit. While He doesn't leave us at that time, and thank God for that, still, we tie His hands, so to speak, by placing our faith in things other than Christ and the Cross.

Most believers have at least some understanding of the Cross of Christ as it refers to salvation. The statement, "Jesus died for me," is perhaps the greatest statement on the face of the earth. However, when it comes to sanctification—how we live for God on a daily, ongoing basis—most Christians don't have the foggiest idea what part the Cross plays in their life and living. And yet, almost everything that Paul wrote in his

14 epistles concerns the sanctification process. Sadly and regrettably, the modern church just simply does not know how the Holy Spirit works.

If they give Him a thought at all, they think that what He does is automatic, but we know that's not true. If the Holy Spirit just did things automatically, there would never be another failure in the life of a Christian. The Holy Spirit would just step in, stop the process, and the Christian would avoid all failure; however, we know that's not true, don't we?

The truth is, there are millions of godly people who truly love the Lord and are being used by God, but at the same time, they're not living victoriously in their own lives, and they don't understand why.

While the Holy Spirit helps them as it regards service for the Lord, due to the fact that their faith is in something other than Christ and the Cross, the Holy Spirit is greatly hindered in the sanctification process. That's a shame because that for which Jesus died not only includes salvation, but, as well, it includes sanctification.

FALSE TEACHERS

Looking at this situation from the other side, Paul wished the false teachers removed because true Christians had been called unto liberty, and they—the false teachers—were abridging and destroying that liberty. Believers are not in subjection to the law of Moses or to anything else that savors of bondage. We are free—free from the servitude of sin and free from subjection to expensive and burdensome rites and customs, which were hopeless situations anyway. We are to remember this as a great and settled principle. So vital a truth and so important is this that it should be maintained, and so great the evil of forgetting it that Paul says he earnestly wishes that all who would reduce believers to that state of servitude would be severely judged.

Freedom or liberty in Christ is the very principle of the Christian calling and the very ground of the Christian standing. That must never be abrogated.

ONE REASON FOR THE INSISTENCE
OF LAW BY THE FALSE TEACHERS

Paul is teaching two things: Freedom from the law and the consequent freedom from sin. Believers are called by God to such freedom. Painstakingly, Paul had argued that this was an indispensable part of the believer's newfound faith in Christ.

His insistence on this freedom (we speak of freedom from the law) quite naturally caused his opponents to fear that he had destroyed the only bulwark or restraint against the tide of pagan immorality, in other words, the impulse to do wrong.

However, what they failed to realize was that the law did not restrain sin in the first place: this is how it fools people.

Its commandments stand out stark and bold, and the believer's efforts to keep these commandments him feel that he is righteous and, consequently, this is what ought to be done. However, the fact is that the believer cannot keep the law within his own strength and ability. Such is impossible due to the depraved fallen nature.

Many believers, knowing they are new creations in Christ Jesus, misunderstand the entire concept of what Paul is teaching. They think that now, because they are saved and Spirit-filled, surely they can obey the commandments. Paul thought the same thing and records his failure in Romans, Chapter 7.

Why cannot the believer keep the law now that he is saved and Spirit-filled? The reason is that the Holy Spirit will not help him, at least in that capacity. The only way these things can be done is by the power of the Holy Spirit. Man, even redeemed man, is unable to do what needs to be done without the Holy Spirit.

The Lord has designed it this way for several reasons. First of all, our dependence must always be on the Lord and not on ourselves.

If the Lord had given the Israelites the power to keep the law, it would only have increased the problem that was already present, and I speak of pride. They had to be shown how insufficient they actually were, which the law grandly carried out.

WHY WON'T THE HOLY SPIRIT HELP THE BELIEVER KEEP THE COMMANDMENTS?

That sounds strange because it would seem that the keeping of the moral law is the very thing the Holy Spirit would help us to do. In fact, He does, but it's in a different way.

The Holy Spirit won't help us keep the commandments for the simple reason that Jesus has already kept them, and He did it perfectly. In fact, He did it on our behalf. So, it is not a question of the commandments being kept. They have already been kept by the true man, the Lord Jesus Christ. So, when we try to keep them and, thereby, make such the object of our faith, we are, in effect, saying that Jesus did not properly keep them, and so we must do what He failed to do. We may not realize that we are doing this, but that's exactly what is being done, and the Holy Spirit will not help anyone do that which is error.

The idea is that the believer is in Christ. He was in Christ when Jesus died on Calvary (Rom. 6:3), and the believer is still in Christ presently. In fact, he will always be *"in Christ"* (Rom. 8:1).

ONCE AGAIN, THE CROSS COMES INTO VIEW

The believer is not trying to finish a particular work but is trusting in a work that is already finished. That's a key point and must not be passed over lightly.

The believer is not trying to finish a work, meaning that what Christ did leaves something to be desired, but is rather trusting in a work that is already finished, total, complete, and everlasting.

Years ago, I preached that the taking of the land of Canaan by Joshua was a type of our Christian experience in that we now have to take the land, spiritually speaking. I was wrong!

The picture of Joshua taking the land, even as it is brought out in the book that bears the name of that patriarch, is not a type of what the Christian must do in his spiritual experience, but rather what Jesus has already done. We Christians must enter into His completed victory. I'm not trying to take any land today; it has already been taken for me. I'm not trying to kill another giant, even as David did, for Jesus, of whom David was a type, has already killed the giant (Satan), and that means that I am free from those conflicts and battles.

To enjoy this, to walk in this victory, and to be the overcomer I already am, all I have to do is trust in what Jesus did at the Cross. I must understand that this is the key to my salvation, and it is, as well, the key to my victory as it regards my everyday walk. Everything is in the Cross. *Everything* is in the Cross!

I WILL GIVE YOU REST

Listen to what Jesus said: *"Come unto Me, all you who labor and are heavy laden, and I will give you rest. Take My yoke upon you, and learn of Me; for I am meek and lowly in heart: and ye shall find rest unto your souls. For My yoke is easy, and My burden is light"* (Mat. 11:28-30).

If one is to notice, Jesus twice said that in our coming to Him, we would find rest. He didn't say that we would come into a battle or a conflict, but rather rest. Admittedly, there is conflict and even war, and no, that is not a contradiction. The conflict and the war come in as it regards our faith. The only fight in which we are to be engaged is the *"good fight of faith"* (I Tim. 6:12).

Faith in what?

We are speaking of faith in what Jesus did at the Cross and the resurrection, understanding that His work is a finished work, and that it includes everything I need to live a victorious, overcoming Christian life. The answer to everything is found in the Cross (I Cor. 1:17-18, 23; 2:2; Rom. 8:1-11; Col. 2:10-15).

It was at the Cross where all victory was won, and it was all done on our behalf. Jesus didn't do what He did at Calvary for God the Father, and neither did He do it for angels. He did it for you and me. We are the ones who owed a debt that we could not pay, and that debt was owed to God. He paid it for us by the giving of Himself as a perfect sacrifice, and it was the only sacrifice that has ever been perfect. God accepted it, and did so in totality. When I came to Christ, and when you came to Christ, we were crucified with Christ, buried with Him, and raised with Him in newness of life (Rom. 6:1-5). That's the key to all things and the answer to all of our questions.

You and I may fail and, in fact, will fail. I don't like to say that, but it is the truth. That we must understand. The Cross does not fail, and, in fact, it cannot fail. So, that means that the new covenant cannot fail, and, actually, the new covenant is Jesus Christ. The Cross of Christ is the meaning of that covenant—the meaning of which was given to the apostle Paul, which he gave to us in his 14 epistles.

AGAIN, HOW DOES THIS WORK AS IT RELATES TO THE HOLY SPIRIT?

I am a strong proponent, actually, as strong as is possible to be, that after coming to Christ, the believing sinner should immediately go on and be baptized with the Holy Spirit with the evidence of speaking with other tongues (Acts 2:4; 10:46; 19:1-7). Actually, the Lord commanded this (Acts 1:4). Without the baptism with the Holy Spirit, which is available to every single believer, all that He needs to do cannot be done. He perfectly states that the moment a person comes to Christ, the Holy Spirit definitely comes within the heart and life of such an individual. However, there is a vast difference between being born of the Spirit and being baptized with the Spirit.

And yet many Spirit-filled believers think that the infilling of the Holy Spirit automatically guarantees all the victory that we need, and then when that doesn't happen, they are very confused. The truth is, the baptism with the Holy Spirit is given to us for service. To be sure, He wants to help us to live a godly, holy life; however, for us to live that holy life, we must understand that He works entirely within the capacity of the Cross. To live a holy life means to have victory over the world, the flesh, and the Devil. The Holy Spirit alone can get this done within our lives. In other words, it's the Cross of Christ that gave and gives the Holy Spirit the legal means to do all that He does within our hearts and lives (Rom. 8:2).

Let me say it this way: There are millions of Christians around the world who truly love God and are being used of God, and some greatly so. However, unless those Christians understand the Cross of Christ relative to our sanctification, despite the fact that God is using them, they cannot live a victorious life. As stated, they can be used of the Lord, and many are, but they aren't living a victorious life within themselves. They may try to make themselves think they are, and they may claim that they are to others, but they really aren't. In fact, it's impossible for a believer to have victory over the world, the flesh, and the Devil unless he understands the part the Cross of Christ plays as it regards his sanctification, in other words, how he is to live for God on a daily basis (Lk. 9:23).

SIN

When it comes to sin, the Cross and the Cross alone answers the question. Every sin was defeated at Calvary's Cross when our Saviour gave Himself as a perfect sacrifice. This means that Satan himself, plus all fallen angels and demon spirits, were defeated at Calvary's Cross. When we were born again, we entered into the great victory won by our Lord (Col. 2:10-15).

SO, WHAT IS THE PROBLEM?

When we mention the problem, we are speaking of the failure to live a victorious life, no matter how hard we try.

The problem is that we have placed our faith in other things, such as fasting, witnessing, giving money to the work of God, being faithful to church, or a hundred other things that one could name. While those things within themselves aren't wrong, for us to place our faith accordingly in those things is an insult to Christ, as we've already stated. Consequently, the Holy Spirit cannot work in such an atmosphere. The truth is, we are being unfaithful to Christ when we do such a thing.

Let me say it again because it is so very, very important: Our faith is to be exclusively in Christ and what He did for us at the Cross. It is to be maintained exclusively in that finished work. Then the Holy Spirit, who works entirely within the capacity of the Cross of Christ, will grandly work on our behalf and give us the victory that we desperately need. What is impossible to us is very easy for Him because the Holy Spirit is God, which means that He can do anything.

Never forget the following: The Holy Spirit works entirely by and through the Cross of Christ.

Let's look at it a little more closely: Before the Cross, the Holy Spirit could not come into the heart and life of any believer to abide permanently. He did enter the hearts and lives of some prophets, etc., but when their work was completed, He would leave. Why would He leave?

The reason is that the blood of bulls and goats could not take away sins. Consequently, the sin debt remained, so that meant that He could not do what He can now do (Heb. 10:4).

As well, when believers died before the Cross, their souls and spirits did not go to heaven, but rather down into paradise. Actually, they became captives of Satan. The Evil One could not hurt them or do anything negative to them, but they were still Satan's captives. However, when Jesus died on the Cross, He went down into paradise and *"led captivity captive."* This means that He made every one of those souls in paradise His captives and, in effect, took them with Him to the portals of glory. Since the Cross, when a believer dies, his soul and spirit immediately go to heaven to be with the Lord (Eph. 4:8-10).

As well, since the Cross, which answered the sin question in totality, the moment the believing sinner comes to Christ, the Holy Spirit comes into that heart and life, there to abide forever (Jn. 14:16). All of this is made possible by the Cross.

The Holy Spirit does not demand very much of us, but He does demand one thing, and on that He will not give or bend, so to speak. He demands that our faith be exclusively in Christ and what Christ has done for us at the Cross.

That's why Paul also said: *"Christ sent me not to baptize, but to preach the gospel: not with wisdom of words, lest the Cross of Christ should be made of none effect"* (I Cor. 1:17).

Paul wasn't knocking water baptism. He was merely stating that the emphasis must always be on the Cross of Christ and never on other things, as important as those other things might be.

When our faith is placed in Christ and His Cross, and maintained exclusively in Christ and the Cross, the Holy Spirit then has the latitude to do within our lives what needs to be done. Never forget that He works exclusively within the Cross, which demands our faith.

SELF-RIGHTEOUSNESS

When the believer attempts to live for God by any means other than faith in Christ and the Cross, no matter what the other direction is or how religious it may be, the end result will always be self-righteousness. It's because, in reality, our faith is actually in ourselves and not really in Christ. As already stated, we must understand that every victory was won at the Cross. All sin was atoned at the Cross. Every demon force of darkness, including Satan himself, was defeated at the Cross. It is a finished work. As someone has readily said, "What is it about the statement 'finished work' that you don't understand?" It is very simple and means exactly what it says.

Whenever we try to place our faith in something other than Christ and the Cross, we are, in essence, saying that what Jesus did at the Cross was not enough, and we have to add our two cents to what He has accomplished. That is an insult to Christ, which the Holy Spirit cannot tolerate. So, if you want the help of the Holy Spirit, you must place your faith exclusively in Christ and the Cross, and maintain it exclusively in such. To be sure, we must have the help of the Holy Spirit if we're going to live the life we ought to live. Then we will have the constant, abiding presence and help of the Holy Spirit, which will give us victory over the world, the flesh, and the Devil (Rom. 6:1-14; 8:1-11; I Cor. 1:17-18, 23; 2:2; Gal. 6:14; Col. 2:10-15).

ENEMIES OF THE CROSS

Listen again to the apostle Paul, and I quote entirely from The Expositor's Study Bible:

(*For many walk* (speaks of those attempting to live for God outside of the victory and rudiments of the Cross of Christ), *of whom I have told you often, and now tell you even weeping* (this is a most serious matter), *that they are the enemies of the Cross of Christ* (those who do not look exclusively to the Cross of Christ must be labeled 'enemies'): *Whose end is destruction* (if the Cross is ignored, and continues to be ignored, the loss of the soul is the only ultimate conclusion), *whose god is their belly* (refers to those who attempt to pervert the gospel for their own personal gain), *and whose glory is in their shame* (the material things they seek, God labels as 'shame'), *who mind earthly things.* (This means they have no interest in heavenly things, which signifies they are using the Lord for their own personal gain) (Phil. 3:18-19).

When the Lord first began to open up this great truth to me, I thought at the time that the reason the Cross was ignored was because of ignorance. In other words, they just didn't know any better, and I speak of preachers and laymen both. I felt that they just simply didn't understand anything much about the Cross, especially as it regarded our sanctification. However, after awhile, I came to believe that the real culprit was and is rank and raw unbelief, even though the ignorance was there. In spite of their ignorance about the Cross, they simply did not believe, and that means that they are enemies of the Cross of Christ.

The reason the modern church has gone headlong into humanistic psychology, which was birthed by Satan, is because of unbelief as it regards the Cross of Christ. They simply do not believe that what Jesus there did is the answer for man's dilemma. When I say that, I'm speaking not only of salvation but our sanctification. When we place our faith in anything other than

Christ and the Cross, meaning that such a thing becomes the object of our faith, the sin nature is then going to rule within our hearts and lives. This makes for a miserable existence. The tragedy is that most modern Christians don't have the slightest idea of what the sin nature is.

The sin nature, or one might like to say, the evil nature, is a result of the fall of Adam in the garden of Eden. When he fell (along with Eve), everything he (they) did then became sin. In fact, every unbeliever in this world today is ruled totally and completely by the sin nature, which is the cause of all problems. The tragedy is that if the believer doesn't understand the Cross of Christ relative to sanctification, as stated, the sin nature is going to rule that believer, which makes for a miserable existence.

In Romans 6, Paul mentions the word *sin* some 17 times, I believe. Sixteen of those times, he is speaking of the sin nature.

This means that when he originally wrote the book of Romans, in front of the word *sin*, he placed what is referred to now as the definite article—the word *the*—making it read *"the* sin." In other words, he was not speaking of acts of sin in Chapter 6, except that one time in verse 15, but is speaking of the sin nature controlling the believer. In fact, Romans 6 tells us how to have victory over the sin nature. While the sin nature is made dormant by the Cross the moment we get saved, it is reactivated if we place our faith in anything except Christ and the Cross. In fact, sin will not reactivate it, but the wrong placement of our faith most definitely will. Then, we've got Christians who are being compelled to go in certain directions that are wrong, meaning they can't stop the sin within their lives, and they don't understand why.

That's why the great apostle Paul said:

> *For that which I do* (the failure) *I allow not* (should have been translated, 'I understand not'; these are not the words of an unsaved man as some claim, but rather a believer who is trying and failing): *for what I would, that do I not* (refers to the obedience he wants to render to Christ, but rather fails; why? As Paul explained, the believer is married to Christ but is being unfaithful to Christ by spiritually cohabiting with the law, which frustrates the grace of God; that means the Holy Spirit will not help such a person, which guarantees failure [Gal. 2:21]); *but what I hate, that do I* (refers to sin in his life, which he doesn't want to do, and, in fact, hates, but finds himself unable to stop; unfortunately, due to the fact of not understanding the Cross as it refers to sanctification, this is the plight of most modern Christians) (Rom. 7:15, The Expositor's Study Bible).

Please understand that Romans 7, as Paul deals with it, is not speaking of his life before his conversion on the road to Damascus, but rather after he was saved, Spirit-filled, and had already begun preaching the gospel. In fact, during all of this time, he was an apostle. However, at a given point in time, the Lord gave Paul the meaning of the new covenant, the meaning of which is the Cross, and that's what he's dealing with in Romans 7.

AN OCCASION TO THE FLESH

The phrase, *"Only use not liberty for an occasion to the flesh,"* actually means, through the word *occasion,* a base of operations. Paul exhorts the Galatians not to make their liberty from the law a base of operations from which to serve sin. That is the sure road to disaster and something, it would seem, that no Christian would desire to do. However, as long as there are human beings, whatever weird thing that can be done will ultimately be done.

In fact, there are untold numbers of Christians who fall into this very category. They are claiming Christianity while, at the same time, living a life of sin. They have in their minds that grace will cover all of their sinning, which, of course, is a travesty.

It is definitely true that the Lord will forgive any time a believer truly seeks such, and He has no limitations on the number of times He will do so. Still, to take sin lightly just because we can be forgiven is insane. No one gets by with sin. Even though God will forgive, sin always leaves its mark in some way because of its deadly power. The idea of all of this is that the Lord does not save *in* sin, but rather *from* sin. In fact, that's what all of this is all about—the Cross of Christ and the sanctification process. Who in the world would want to keep on sinning?

The idea of all of this is that you are called to liberty, but it is not liberty for an occasion to the flesh. It is not freedom from virtuous restraints and from the laws of God. It is liberty from the servitude of sin and religious rites and ceremonies. It is not freedom from the necessary restraints of virtue. This is necessary for several reasons:

1. *Licentiousness.* There is a strong tendency in some converts to relapse again into their former habits. Licentiousness abounds everywhere. Where one has been addicted to certain things before their conversion, considering that most are still surrounded by it on every hand, there is always the danger of falling into it again, whatever it might be. Consequently, the liberty spoken of here by Paul needs to be explained, even as he has done.

2. *Antinomianism.* As the history of the church has shown, there has been a strong tendency to abuse the doctrine of grace. The doctrine that Christians are free and that there is liberty to them from restraint has been perverted by antinomians, and has been made the occasion of their indulging freely in sin. The result has shown that nothing was more important than to guard the doctrine of Christian liberty, and to show exactly what Christians are freed from, and what laws are still binding on them. Paul is, therefore, at great pains to show that the doctrines that he had maintained did not lead to licentiousness and did not allow the indulgence of sinful and corrupt passions. *Antinomianism* means "the conflicting of laws." In other words, the law of sin is indulged but thought to be overcome by the law of grace, that is, if one would use such terminology in that capacity. Such is a perversion of the truth and, actually, the opposite intended by the Holy Spirit. In fact, the doctrine of once saved always saved encourages this perversion.

The thrust of all of this is that the believer's freedom results in a release from the compulsive grip and power of sin. They are no longer controlled by the sinful nature (forced to live by it).

However, the abuse of their freedom would provide an occasion (opportunity) for sin to regain its control over them.

BY LOVE

The phrase, *"But by love serve one another"* (Gal. 5:13), presents the safeguard against such an abuse of freedom, not in its denial through compulsive slavery of legalism, but in a new voluntary slavery of love—by love serve one another.

Here is the vital and revealing paradox that we have previously mentioned. They were admonished to voluntarily enslave themselves to each other. They were free, yet, to remain free, they must enslave themselves again (Rom. 6:15-22; I Cor. 9:19). This is Paul's constant concern. How will you use your freedom? How will you live your new life?

The new slavery, if one would use such a phrase, was and is possible through love (agape). The context reveals that the significance of *agape* is "clearly that of benevolence, desire for the well-being of others, leading to efforts on their behalf." The idea is that the man in Christ is liberated to love.

This certainly harmonizes with Paul's consistent teaching. When coupled with Galatians 5:15, it becomes clear that the threatened abuse of their freedom was in the area of personal relationships.

Thus, Paul strongly denied that his rejection of works eliminated the dynamic for moral and ethical conduct. Instead, it provided the very opposite. True faith finds its expression in love. Thus, it is further seen in the important fact that agape is not mere human sentiment; it is the love of God that has been poured out in the believer's heart (Rom. 5:5).

Such love destroys the desire for that which is evil. So, as it regards the tendency to do wrong, a person might look at himself and ask, "How much do I really love the Lord?" because true love does not want to offend the very one whom we claim to love the most.

LOVE AS USED HERE

As we've already stated, the love spoken of here by Paul is agape love, which refers not to human affection but divine love. That is the love produced in the heart of the yielded believer by the Holy Spirit, and the love with which the believer should love his fellow believers. Please understand that if we love God like we should, we will at the same time love our fellow believer.

This love is a love whose chief essence is self-sacrifice for the benefit of the one who is loved. Such a love means death to self, and that means defeat for sin since the essence of sin is self-will and self-gratification.

The word *serve*, as Paul uses it here, means "to render service to, to do that which is for the advantage of someone else." In fact, it is the word Paul used when he spoke of the slavery that is imposed by the law upon the one who is under law.

The Galatian Christians were rescued from the slavery that legalism imposed and brought into a new servitude. That servitude was that of a loving, glad, and willing service to God and man that annihilates self and subordinates all selfish desires to love.

The secret to victory over sin is our faith in the Cross, which ensures the help of the Holy Spirit, and the result of that victory will be our love for God and others. Actually, the greatest way to show love for God is for love to be shown for others.

In other words, we do loving and kind things for our fellow believers, not because there is a law that says we must do such, but because we truly and sincerely love them and desire to do these things. That's because of the new nature that is now within us. It is the God-nature. Isn't that beautiful?

Going back to Galatians 5:6, this is the faith that works by love.

THE LAW

"For all the law is fulfilled in one word, even in this; You shall love your neighbor as yourself" (Gal. 5:14).

Throughout this letter Paul has been arguing against law and in defense of the gospel of pure grace—the Cross. Now, in a most striking fashion, he returns to law and seems to speak favorably of it, stressing that when Christians love and serve others, the law is fulfilled.

There is a play here on two meanings of the Greek word *peplodrotar*, translated "summed up." On the one hand, it refers to the fact that the law can aptly be summarized by the words of

Leviticus 19:18. This idea was commonplace in the time of Christ, and Jesus endorsed it in Matthew 22:39 and Luke 10:25-28.

On the other hand, the word can also mean "fulfilled" (as in Romans 13:8). In this, Paul is suggesting that it is actually out of the new life of love made possible within the Christian community through the Spirit that the law finds fulfillment.

THE FULFILLMENT OF THE LAW

The phrase, *"For all the law is fulfilled in one word, even in this,"* presents the apostle telling us how that the law is fulfilled in our lives. The apostle has up to this point bent all his efforts at dissuading the Galatians from coming under bondage to law again. Now he exhorts them to love one another. If they do this, he says, they will fulfill the law. How are we to understand this?

In Romans 8:4, Paul speaks of the fact that the righteousness of the law is fulfilled in the Christian by the Holy Spirit. There is, therefore, a sense in which the word *law* is used other than in the legalistic sense in which Paul has used it throughout this letter so far. It is that sense in which it is conceived of as divine law consisting of ethical principles and standards that inhere in the being of God, and represent those things that go to make up right conduct on the part of man.

ALL THAT THE MOSAIC LAW REQUIRES

Paul's statement becomes intelligible and consistent when we recognize the following points:

- Believers, through their new relation to the Lord Jesus, are released from the whole law as statutes and from the obligation to obey its statutes.
- All that God's law requires—as an expression of His will—is included in love.
- When the believer acts on the principle of love, he is fulfilling in his actions toward God, his fellowman, and himself all that the Mosaic law would require of him in his position in life, were that law in force.

The statutes of the law, the believer will obey, so far as love itself requires such a course of action from him. In no case will he obey them as statutes, but rather as a believer in Christ, who is like Christ, with Christ actually performing the work through the believer. It is all done by the power of the Holy Spirit (Gal. 2:20). Of course, when we speak of law now as it regards the believer, we are speaking of the moral aspect of the law, in effect, the Ten Commandments.

Thus, the individual is released from one law and is brought under another law. The first law consisted of a set of ethical principles to which was attached blessing for obedience and punishment for disobedience. It was a law, incidentally, that gave him neither the desire nor the power to obey its commands.

The second law is the law of love. This is not a set of written commandments but an ethical and a spiritual dynamic that is produced by the Holy Spirit in the heart of the yielded believer. He gives him both the desire and the power to live a life in which the dominating principle is love—God's love.

This love exercises a stronger and stricter control over the heart, and it is far more efficient at putting out sin in the life than the thunders of Sinai ever could.

THE CROSS AND THE LOVE OF GOD

Inasmuch as the Cross was the greatest exhibition of love that man has ever known and, in fact, will ever know, this serves as the basis of all that the believer is to be in Christ Jesus. If the believer starts out with the Cross, he must start out with love, for there is no other recourse or direction. With faith in the Cross a dominating factor in the life of the believer, love is the natural outflow. As well, it will be a love that is never condescending but always from the heart of the person to the heart of the one loved. It is to the highest aspect of Christianity that the Holy Spirit is constantly prodding us, and it provides the most fulfilling, rewarding life there could ever be. This is what the world talks about but, actually, can never attain to its glory because such comes only from God. In fact, it is not possible in an unregenerate human heart.

LOVE YOUR NEIGHBOR AS YOURSELF

The phrase, *"You shall love your neighbor as yourself,"* is summed up in the word *fulfilled* that is used in the first phrase. It is taken from the Greek *pleroo,* which means "to make full," and when used of a task or a course of action, it means "to fully perform" or "to fully obey."

The idea is that in this, the whole law stands fully obeyed.

The idea is not that the whole law is embraced in or summed up in the act of loving one's neighbor as oneself, but that in doing this, one is complying with the whole law and its demands.

With great skill, the apostle changes the subject from a doctrinal argument to a strain of practical remarks. He furnishes most important lessons for the right mode of overcoming our corrupt and sensual passions and discharging our duty to others.

At first glance, Paul's statement appears to contradict all that he has laboriously argued with reference to works of righteousness. If the law had only a temporary function that was abrogated by the coming of Christ, why should the believer be concerned about fulfilling the law?

There is no doubt that Paul uses law in two different ways, but this must not be construed to mean that the term intrinsically has contradictory meanings. In Romans and Galatians, where Paul is combating the Judaizers, he uses the term in the sense that his opponents used it, namely, a legalistic system.

When Paul uses the word in this manner, it is necessary to understand it as an effort to find salvation through good deeds—works of righteousness— which cannot be done. To such works of law, the believer is dead (Rom. 7:4, 6).

On the other hand, Paul's understanding of law in its basic sense as the divine standard has binding requirements on all men, as should be obvious. These requirements, however, can be met or fulfilled only through Christ (Rom. 8:4). In fact, the love (agape) that Paul admonishes the Galatians to express is not human. It is rather the love of God and the fruit of the Spirit.

THE LAW AS IT TOUCHES THE CHRISTIAN PRESENTLY

The whole law with all of its requirements is fulfilled through the love of God as it is expressed in the believer's life. In fact, in many newer translations, the word *fulfilled* is replaced by "summed up." The reason for this is the parallel passage in Romans 13:9, *"If there be any other commandment, it is briefly comprehended* (summed up) *in this saying, namely, You shall love your neighbor as yourself."* In the Romans passage, it should be noted, however, that it is the commandments, some of which Paul had just listed, that are summed up in the Great Commandment. Even in this context (Rom. 13:8-10), the apostle makes it clear that love is the fulfillment of the law. Thus, even though the commandments are summed up in the Great Commandment, the whole law is satisfied or fulfilled in love.

This simply means that all of the requirements of the law of God are fully obeyed through love. It is clear then that the Christian is not excused from the requirements of the law. God cannot smile on those who do what He forbids; however, such obedience is not the means of obtaining salvation but the result of salvation, i.e., the gift of His grace—the Holy Spirit.

Inasmuch as Paul has pretty well summed up holy living in the one word—love—let's look at this situation a little closer.

LOVE IS THE ANSWER

"What shall we say then? Shall we continue in sin, that grace may abound? God forbid. How shall we, who are dead to sin, live any longer therein?" (Rom. 6:1-2).

The apostle Paul anticipated many questions that would be raised by his teaching of the grace of God and freedom from the law for believers. He had taught that the believer in Christ is *"delivered"* from the law (Rom. 7:6); *"dead"* to the law (Gal. 2:19); and *"redeemed"* from the curse of the law (Gal. 3:13). He had shown that the sinner cannot be saved by the works of the law and that the believer cannot be kept by the works of the law. Again and again, he repeats that the believer is *"not under the law, but under grace"* (Rom. 6:14-15).

The legalists of his day were quick to accuse Paul of preaching a dangerous gospel. They followed him everywhere in order to undo his preaching of grace. These attacks have continued to this day against all who teach deliverance from the law by faith.

Now, we do not teach that the law is not active today in declaring God's righteousness and condemning the sinner, for it is. However, we do teach that those who trust in the finished work of Christ are not only redeemed from the curse and the penalty, but from the law itself. A law without penalties is powerless, and since the penalty of the law was fully borne by Christ, the believer is forever delivered from its power.

We shall try to answer some of the objections that are raised, constantly, against this doctrine of grace to save and grace to keep.

DOES THIS LIBERTY GIVE A LICENSE TO SIN?

It is persistently argued by the legalists that the teaching of absolute grace in salvation leads to looseness and carelessness in living. To teach the security of the believer by grace is condemned by some critics as an encouragement to sin and is even called by some a "damnable doctrine." Of course, those who say these things are actually attempting to live for Christ by law, which the Holy Spirit through Paul roundly condemns.

Irrespective, when we preach freedom from the law, we are accused of being lawless when, as a matter of fact, we are far more under law after we are saved than before. However, it is under a different law and a more powerful law—the law of love instead of the law of commandments. The true believer seeks to keep the law of God, but it is from an entirely different motive. The believer is still obligated to observe God's law, and I speak of the moral law, but it is now kept in a far different manner. It is not as an effort to keep oneself saved or out of fear of punishment.

The believer has a moral obligation to live a holy life, not because the law demands it, but because grace produces it. To say, therefore, that freedom from the law makes one lawless is to show complete ignorance of both the ministry of the law and the power of the grace of God. The only service a believer can render that is pleasing to God must be generated by a grateful love for our deliverance. Any service motivated by an effort to escape punishment or fear of losing salvation is wholly rejected by the Lord. The believer must live under the spirit of the law, not by the letter of the law.

The believer is under a new law given to us by the Lord Jesus Himself. It is indeed called "the law of Christ." It is the law of love in contrast to the law of commandments. Paul says in Galatians 2:19, *"I … Am dead to the law, that I might live unto God."*

THE LAW OF LOVE

In speaking to His disciples in John, Chapter 15, Jesus says, *"If you keep My commandments, you shall abide in My love; even as I have kept My Father's commandments, and abide in His love"* (Jn. 15:10).

What commandments is Jesus talking about? He certainly is not speaking of the Ten Commandments as so many imagine. He is speaking about a different law of commandments and explains it in verse 12: *"This is My commandment, That you love one another, as I have loved you"* (Jn. 15:12).

This is called by Paul the "law of Christ." He said, *"Bear ye one another's burdens, and so fulfill the law of Christ"* (Gal. 6:2).

The law of Christ is the law of love and the fruit of the new nature and the Spirit of God. Let us quote it again: *"For all the law is fulfilled in one word, even in this; You shall love your neighbor as yourself"* (Gal. 5:14).

The apostle John, in writing to believers, said, *"And whatsoever we ask, we receive of Him, because we keep His commandments, and do those things that are pleasing in His sight"* (I Jn. 3:22).

What commandments is John talking about? He certainly was not speaking of the Ten Commandments, for he immediately adds: *"And this is His commandment, That we should believe on the name of His Son Jesus Christ, and love one another, as He gave us commandment"* (I Jn. 3:23).

We might go on and on to show that while we are delivered from the law of commandments given by Moses, we are not left without law. We are not lawless but are placed under another higher, more glorious law—the law of love, called also the *"perfect law of liberty"* (James 1:25).

Let us mention one more Scripture that climaxes it all. Paul said, *"Love is the fulfilling of the law"* (Rom. 13:10).

LOVE, THE FULFILLING OF THE LAW

Where love is the motive for service, no laws, rules, or regulations are ever needed. To use an illustration, imagine a man employing a servant. To avoid any trouble or misunderstanding, certain rules and conditions must be agreed upon. The employer hands to his prospective employee a manual in which the relationship of employer and servant are set forward. The employer agrees to pay a certain amount of wages per week, with provision for sick pay, vacation, coffee breaks, proper working conditions, and other fringe benefits. The servant or employee agrees to work 40 hours a week, be at work at the appointed time, and produce a certain amount of work. They sit down at a bargaining session, and agreement is reached. Failure to abide by the rules would break the contract, and the employee will either go on strike, or the boss will fire him, as the case may be. The responsibilities of both employer and employee have been spelled out in detail. The servant is under law—he received his wages and benefits upon condition of meeting all the responsibilities mentioned and demanded in the contract.

LOVE STEPS IN

Now, let us suppose this employee is a young lady and, in the course of events, the boss—a bachelor—falls in love with his servant. Finally, they decide to marry, and they become husband and wife. She quits her job (not her work), and they move into their new home. The very moment she becomes the wife, she ceases to be a servant. She is no longer under rules, regulations, and laws. She is not handed an employee's manual to tell her what is expected of her as a wife. She is in love with her husband and he with her, and now she does as much, and even far more, to please her husband as when he was her boss. She is no longer under law—she does not punch a clock, and she has no set of rules to observe. She is free—free to spend all of her time pleasing her husband. No demands are made upon her, for she already anticipates all her husband's wishes. She is no more a servant and no more under laws, rules, and regulations. Does this make her careless and say, "Now that I am not anymore under law, I can do as I please?" No! She is under the law of love.

CAN YOU IMAGINE ...

Love is the fulfilling of the law. Where love reigns, no laws are needed. Can you imagine the husband of this wife posting a set of 10 commandments on the wall of the kitchen to remind his wife constantly of her responsibility to him? Can you imagine this wife faced each morning with the following set of laws posted above the kitchen sink:

"Ten Commandments for My Wife"
- You shall entertain no other husbands beside me.
- You shall not have pictures, photographs, or mementos of other men for you to worship.
- You shall not take my name in vain or speak disparagingly about me.
- You shall not sweep the dirt under the rug.
- You shall faithfully prepare my meals, see that my laundry is taken care of, etc.

The list goes all the way down—10 commandments.

No, a loving wife does not even have to be reminded of these things, for love anticipates all the needs of her husband and all of her needs regarding him. She does not have certain working hours, and she does not receive wages, although she is on duty 24 hours of the day. The husband does not have to say to her, "These are your responsibilities. See that you perform them perfectly, for if you don't, I will punish you or even divorce you." The whole thing is silly. Love makes such a situation unthankful.

THE MORE LOVE, THE LESS LAW

A servant is only expected to do as much as is legally required and only as much as the contract covers, but it is not so with a faithful wife. She goes far beyond what a servant does. So, too, when we are saved by grace and we come under the law of Christ, which is the law of love, we not only seek to do all that we were required to do under the law of a servant, but we go far beyond the demands of the law. The loving wife does not say, "Well, I've done all I am required to do. I've put in my time. Now I am free." Instead, this service of love knows no limits.

Love, then, is the fulfilling of the law. The more love, the less law; and the less love, the more law is needed. All the requirements of the law are met where love rules and controls.

Listen to Paul in Romans, Chapter 13:

Owe no man anything, but to love one another: for he who loves another has fulfilled the law. For this, You shall not commit adultery, You shall not kill, You shall not steal, You shall not bear false witness, You shall not covet; and if there be any other commandment, it is briefly comprehended in this saying, namely, You shall love your neighbor as yourself. Love works no ill to his neighbor: therefore love is the fulfilling of the law (Rom. 13:8-10).

This same thing was expressed by Jesus in Matthew 19:19 and Mark 12:31, and repeated by Paul in Galatians 5:14: *"For, brethren, you have been called unto liberty; only use not liberty for an occasion to the flesh, but by love serve one another. For all the law is fulfilled in one word, even in this; You shall love your neighbor as yourself"* (Gal. 5:13-14).

Where this tenet of love is practiced, there is no more need for any laws. You could discharge every police officer and close every court of law. If you love the Lord God with all of your heart, mind, and soul and your neighbor as yourself, the law has no power over you. If you love your neighbor as yourself, you will not commit adultery with his wife. If you love your neighbor as yourself, you will not kill him. If you love your neighbor as yourself, you will not steal from him. If you love your neighbor as yourself, you will not bear false witness against him. If you love your neighbor as yourself, you will not covet what belongs to him. Again, says Paul:

"If there be any other commandment, it is briefly comprehended in this saying, namely, You shall love your neighbor as yourself" (Rom. 13:9).

Brother, may I ask you, "Are you under the law of commandments, or are you motivated by the law of love?" You say, "Who is sufficient unto these things? My love is so imperfect, often so cold, and I come so far short. When I fail to be motivated by perfect love, do I bend then again under the law of condemnation and the curse?"

Bless God, no, for He knew our frailty and made provision by His grace for even this, and we repeat once more I John 2:1 and I John 1:8-10:

- *"My little children, these things write I unto you, that you sin not. And* (but) *if any man sin, we have an advocate with the Father, Jesus Christ the righteous"* (I Jn. 2:1).
- *"If we say that we* (believers) *have no sin* (sin nature), *we deceive ourselves, and the truth is not in us."*
- *"If we confess our sins, He is faithful and just to forgive us our sins, and to cleanse us from all unrighteousness."*

- *"If we say that we have not sinned, we make Him a liar, and His Word is not in us"* (I Jn. 1:8-10).

CANNIBAL CHRISTIANS

"But if you bite and devour one another, take heed that you be not consumed one of another" (Gal. 5:15).

It is not hard to imagine the kind of strife that may have been present in the Galatian churches – either strife parallel to that of the Corinthians (I Cor. 1:10-12; 3:1-4) or strife arising directly out of the conflict with the legalizers. Paul does not say precisely what it was, but so far as Paul knew, it was even then existing, as is evident from the tense of these verbs as they are given in the Greek. That it was intense seems evident from the sentence structure and, as well, by the fact that they moved by increasingly strong degrees to a climax.

The phrase, *"But if you bite and devour one another,"* presents the words *bite* and *devour* as used commonly in classical Greek in connection with wild animals in a deadly struggle. It means that such a condition was existing even then in the Galatian churches.

Wuest says, "Neither the passage itself nor the context tells us in so many words to what this condition of strife was due. But most probably it was strife over matters on which the Judaizers were unsettling them. The words constitute a strong expression of partisan hatred resulting in actions that lead to neutral injury."

The ever-practical Paul applies the principle of love to what was obviously the urgent problem at that time in Galatia. Evidently, the Judaizers had not convinced all of Paul's converts.

The result was grievous strife between the two factions. This undoubtedly hurt Paul more than all else – to see his beloved converts destroying each other. There is certainly no sadder picture in any church in any day. The only adequate remedy is love that causes one to serve rather than to consume his fellowman.

The only thing that is worse than a dead church is a fighting, quarrelling church.

TO CONSUME ONE ANOTHER

The phrase, *"Take heed that you be not consumed one of another,"* along with *bite* and *devour,* point to complete and utter devastation.

Consumed in the Greek is *analisko* and means "to use them, to destroy." The implication here is that such activity could ultimately cause the loss of their souls.

The idea is that to stress salvation by works tends to promote controversy, which is generally about what one can and cannot do as far as the law is concerned. As stated, love lays all of this aside; consequently, if love is absent, that means the Cross is absent. Fighting and quarrelling always follow the law.

So, it should be fairly easy to know which churches are law churches and which are Cross churches.

I am waiting for the dawning
Of the bright and blessed day,
When the darksome night of sorrow
Shall have vanished far away:
When forever with the Saviour,
Far beyond this vale of tears,
I shall swell the song of worship
Through the everlasting years.

I am looking at the brightness
See, it shines from afar;
Of the clear and joyous beaming
Of the bright and morning star,
Through the dark grey mist of morning
Do I see its glorious light,
Then away with every shadow
Of this sad and weary night.

I am waiting for the coming
Of the Lord who died for me;
Oh His words have thrilled my spirit,
I will come again for Thee,
I can almost hear His footfall,
On the threshold of the door,
And my heart, my heart is longing
To be with Him evermore.

THE YOKE OF BONDAGE

CHAPTER 5

WALK IN THE SPIRIT

WALK IN THE SPIRIT

"THIS I SAY THEN, Walk in the Spirit, and you shall not fulfill the lust of the flesh" (Gal. 5:16).

THIS I SAY THEN ...

What is the solution to such biting, devouring, and destroying that is all too common among Christian assemblies? The answer, Paul says, is living by the Spirit. Then, and only then, will one cease to gratify the desires of the flesh. It is the Holy Spirit alone who can keep the believer truly free, and He does so by the believer taking to himself, by faith, the benefits of the Cross. The Holy Spirit works entirely by and through the Cross of Christ. In other words, it is the Cross—actually what Jesus there did—that gives the Holy Spirit the latitude and the legal means to do all that He does. It is called *"the law of the Spirit of life in Christ Jesus"* (Rom. 8:2).

The contrast between the word *sarx* (flesh) on the one hand and the word *pneuma* (Spirit) on the other is one of the characteristic themes in the New Testament and particularly Pauline theology. It is as important, for instance, as the contrast between the works of the law and the hearing of faith, which has thus far dominated Paul's statement in his letter to the Galatians.

In the earliest days of the Greek language, the word *sarx* mostly meant "the soft, fleshy parts of the body," like its Hebrew equivalent word *basar*; however, sarx soon came to denote the body as a whole, that is, the material part of a person. After that, by extension, it meant the whole man as conditioned by a bodily existence and by natural desires. In other words, it is what a human being can do as it regards motivation, education, talent, ability, personal strength, etc.

In this sense, it is not bad, but when the word was taken over into the Christian vocabulary, as it was to a large degree by Paul, it came to mean man as a fallen being whose desires, even at best, originate from sin and are stained by it. Thus, the word *sarx* came to mean "all the evil that man is and is capable of apart from the intervention of God's grace in his life."

In this respect, the word *sarx* is synonymous with the natural man or the old nature. As it regards the believer and spiritual things, the flesh is anything that is not born of the Spirit of God. In fact, when a believer tries to live for God or do anything for the Lord by the means of the flesh, he is doomed to failure.

THE HOLY SPIRIT

In distinctly spiritual terminology, it is the Spirit of God who takes up residence in Christians to enable us to understand spiritual things (I Cor. 2:14), receive Christ as Saviour and Lord, call God "Father" (Rom. 8:15; Gal. 4:6), and develop a Christian personality. In many characteristic passages, the Holy Spirit is thus the presence of God in believing man through which fellowship with God is made possible, and power is given for winning the warfare against sin in the soul. It comes by the means of the believer placing his or her faith exclusively in Christ and the Cross, which then gives the Holy Spirit the latitude to work within our lives. In other words, the Holy Spirit does everything through the Cross of Christ and thereby demands that Christ and the Cross ever be the object of our faith.

The Holy Spirit is not natural to man in his fallen state, but this does not mean that by the gift of the Spirit the redeemed man escapes the need to place his faith in Christ and the Cross. In a sense, one might say that the Holy Spirit makes victory possible, but only to the degree that the believer lives by the Spirit or walks in Him. The word *walk* implies a necessity of choice.

WALK IN THE SPIRIT

The phrase, *"This I say then, Walk in the Spirit,"* is intended to counteract the erroneous impression held by the Galatians (no doubt, at the suggestion of the Judaizers) that without the restraining influence of the law, they would fall into sin. Instead of an attempt at law, obedience in their own strength motivated by the terrors of the law, Paul rather admonished them to continue to govern their lives by the inward leading of the

Holy Spirit. The type of life and the method of living that life, of which he speaks here, Paul had already commended to them in Galatians 5:5 in the words, *"For we through the Spirit wait for the hope of righteousness."*

Thus, the secret of victory over sin is found not in attempted obedience to a law that has been abrogated, but in subjection to a divine person—the Holy Spirit. At the moment the sinner places his faith in the Lord Jesus, the Holy Spirit takes up His permanent residence in the believer's being for the purpose of ministering to his spiritual needs. This is done as the believer manifests constant dependence on the Cross of Christ, for there is the secret of all victory (I Cor. 1:17-18; 2:2; Col. 2:10-15).

In this context, the word *spirit* refers to neither the human spirit nor the Divine Spirit considered independent of each other, but to the Divine Spirit (Holy Spirit) as He indwells the human spirit. The believer's inner man is thus to be under the motivating, empowering force of the Holy Spirit. This is in diametric contrast to his former life, which was motivated by the desires of the flesh.

THE RESPONSIBILITIES OF THE BELIEVER

Every believer must understand that we are up against forces in the spirit world that are much more powerful than we are. Consequently, if we do not contest these things God's way, we will lose the conflict.

Paul said, *"For we wrestle not against flesh and blood, but against principalities, against powers, against the rulers of the darkness of this world, against spiritual wickedness in high places"* (Eph. 6:12). These are fallen angels and demon spirits. So, how do we face these things? How do we overcome them?

Many believers have it in their minds that the work of the Holy Spirit is automatic. In other words, He does what needs to be done. Nothing could be further from the truth.

Were that the case, there would never be a single failure as it regards any believer. The Holy Spirit would just step in and stop the wrong direction or whatever, and there would be no failure. But we know that's not the case, don't we? So the question is, How does the Holy Spirit work within our lives?

First of all, we must understand that the Holy Spirit is God. As such, He can do anything. In other words, He is all powerful. However, the truth is that He works within certain parameters, and He will not work outside of those parameters. What are they?

It is the Cross of Christ that gives the Holy Spirit the legal means to do all that He does. Listen again to Paul, and I quote from The Expositor's Study Bible:

For the law (that which we are about to give is a law of God, devised by the Godhead in eternity past [I Pet. 1:18-20]; this law, in fact, is 'God's prescribed order of victory') *of the Spirit* (Holy Spirit, i.e., 'the way the Spirit works') *of life* (all life comes from Christ but through the Holy Spirit [Jn. 16:13-14]) *in Christ Jesus* (any time Paul uses this term or one of its derivatives, he is, without fail, referring to what Christ did at the Cross, which makes this 'life' possible) *has made me free* (given me total victory) *from the law of sin and death* (these are the two most powerful laws in the universe; the "law of the Spirit of life in Christ Jesus" alone is stronger than the "law of sin and death"; this means that if the believer attempts to live for God by any manner other than faith in Christ and the Cross, he is doomed to failure) (Rom. 8:2).

So, the believer is to place his or her faith exclusively in Christ and the Cross, and maintain it exclusively in Christ and the Cross. In other words, the Cross of Christ makes everything possible.

Once again, Paul speaks: *"For Christ sent me not to baptize* (presents to us a cardinal truth), *but to preach the gospel* (the manner in which one may be saved from sin): *not with wisdom of words* (intellectualism is not the gospel), *lest the Cross of Christ should be made of none effect.* (This tells us in no uncertain terms that the Cross of Christ must always be the emphasis of the message)" (I Cor. 1:17).

In this one verse, Paul tells us what the gospel actually is, and he warns us about placing emphasis in anything except Christ and the Cross.

SPIRITUAL ADULTERY

If the believer places his or her faith in anything except Christ and the Cross, irrespective of how religious the other thing may be, such a person is being unfaithful to Christ and is actually committing the sin of spiritual adultery.

Paul tells us that we are married to Christ (Rom. 7:1-4; II Cor. 10:1-4). As such, Christ is to meet our every need and, in fact, is the only one who can meet our every need.

To have those needs met, whatever they might be, our faith is to ever be in Christ and what Christ did for us at the Cross. We must understand that every single victory was won at the Cross. There Jesus atoned for all sin—past, present, and future—at least for those who will believe (Jn. 3:16). His atoning for all sin pulled Satan's teeth so to speak. Sin is the legal right that Satan has to hold man captive. With that legal right removed, which was done at Calvary (Col. 2:10-15), Satan has no power to hold anyone captive. The reason that unbelievers and believers alike are in bondage of some sort—if, in fact, the believer is in bondage—is because they will not take advantage of what our Lord has done for them at Calvary's Cross. While the Bible does not teach sinless perfection, it most definitely does teach that sin is not to have dominion over us (Rom. 6:14). If the believer has his or her faith in anything except Christ and the Cross, to be sure, such a person is being dominated by the sin nature. All of this constitutes spiritual adultery.

The Lord has made a way for us, and that way is the Cross. If we look to any other source, irrespective of how scriptural the other source might be in its own right, the Lord looks at our action as spiritual adultery. To be sure, this greatly hinders the Holy Spirit. While He, thank God, doesn't leave us, still, proverbially speaking, we tie His hands when we place our faith in anything other than Christ and the Cross.

THE HOLY SPIRIT KNOWS

Everything that Jesus did at the Cross is known fully by the Holy Spirit. This pertains to everything that was lost in the fall and purchased back in the atonement. It speaks of the sin debt being paid, the grip of sin being broken, cleansing from all sin, power over every sin and demon spirit, and, in fact, power over Satan in every conceivable way. It also refers to the individual growing into a new man, in other words, a new person in Christ Jesus, made in the heavenly image (I Cor. 15:49; Col. 3:10). Consequently, the believer's constant faith in the Cross and dependence on the Spirit guarantee all the benefits purchased and paid for by Jesus Christ and brought to pass in our lives by the person and agency of the Holy Spirit.

WALK

The word *walk* in the Greek is *peripateo*, which means literally "to walk about," but when used in a connection like this, it refers to the act of conducting oneself or ordering one's manner of life or behavior. This speaks of our everyday living for God, our living as an overcomer, and our walk as it regards victory on a daily basis.

The word *walk* may be used in a strictly literal sense, but it is also used figuratively, even as Paul uses it here, to indicate one's lifestyle. Believers once walked in the ways of the world (Col. 3:7), but now we can walk in the light (I Jn. 1:7), in love and obedience (II Jn., v. 6), and in the truth (II Jn., v. 4; III Jn., vs. 3-4).

The way that Paul uses the word here, it pertains to our daily existence, our progress, or the lack thereof. As it regards the Christian, this is what it's all about. How is your walk?

We are told here to walk in the Spirit, which means to do the bidding of the Spirit. This refers to placing our faith exclusively in Christ and what Christ has done for us at the Cross (Rom. 6:3-14; 8:1-11; I Cor. 1:17-18, 23; 2:2; Gal. 6:14; Col. 2:10-15).

Placing our faith entirely in Christ and the Cross constitutes walking in the Spirit. This is the way the Holy Spirit operates, and He will operate no other way.

THE LUST OF THE FLESH

The phrase, *"And you shall not fulfill the lust of the flesh,"* refers to the manner in which Satan tempts the believer. It is through his physical body and the five senses.

- The spirit of man is that which corresponds with God.
- The soul of man is that which corresponds with self.
- The physical body of man is that which corresponds with the world.

The flesh, as used here, has nothing to do with the physical body in the sense of the meat on the bones, although it does have to do with the five senses and those senses desiring things that are not of God. This is the manner in which Satan works on the human being.

He presents things to the five senses that are unholy, ungodly, and referred to as "lusts."

The word *lust* in the Greek is *epithumia,* which refers to "a strong desire, impulse, or passion," with the context indicating whether it is a good or an evil one. The word *flesh* here refers to the totally depraved nature of the person, the power of which is broken when the believer is saved.

The *"lust of the flesh"* refers to the evil desires, impulses, and passions that are constantly arising from the evil nature as smoke rises from a chimney. The evil nature in a believer is not eradicated. However, its power over the believer is broken, that is, if the believer places his or her faith constantly in Christ and the Cross and maintains it accordingly. With that being done, the sin nature will not be able to dominate us. It is all dependent on our faith, and more particularly, the object of our faith, which must ever be Christ and the Cross.

THE WILLPOWER OF THE BELIEVER

Regrettably, most Christians believe that once they give their hearts to Christ, the Lord gives them a "super will." They assume that they are now able to say no to sin, whereas they were not able to do that before conversion. That is not correct.

The willpower of the believer is no stronger than the willpower of the unredeemed. While the will is definitely important—*"whosoever will"*—still, one cannot live for God while meaning to throw off the powers of darkness by willpower. It simply cannot be done that way.

As it regards the will, the believer must *will* the will of God and must cooperate with the Holy Spirit in obtaining that will, which refers to the believer anchoring his faith in Christ and the Cross.

Man is a free moral agent, and as such, God honors man's will and purposely limits Himself so as not to infringe upon the free moral agency of man.

However, as far as the will of man is concerned (of course, we are speaking here of believers), he is never to think that these things can be brought about in his life by the means of willpower. While it definitely requires the will of man in cooperation with the Lord, that's as far as man can go.

As well, if the believer's faith is in the wrong direction, in other words, not centered upon the Cross and what Jesus did there on behalf of sinners, Satan can override the will of the believer and literally force him to do things he does not want to do. That may come as a shock to most believers, for most have been taught, erroneously I might quickly add, that once they come to Jesus, Satan cannot force them to do anything.

He certainly cannot if our faith is in the right place; however, with that not being the case, even as it is with many Christians, Satan can actually force the will of a Christian against what he desires to do. Paul brought this out very succinctly in Romans 7. He said, *"For I know that in me (that is, in my flesh,) dwells no good thing: for to will is present with me; but how to perform that which is good I find not"* (Rom. 7:18).

He then said, *"For I delight in the law of God after the inward man: But I see another law in my members, warring against the law of my mind, and bringing me into captivity to the law of sin which is in my members* (my physical body)*"* (Rom. 7:22-23).

PAUL

Some may attempt to pass this off as Paul's experience before salvation; however, that is patently incorrect. The terminology registered in Romans 7 is not the terminology and experience of a man without God, but rather one who loves the Lord and hates sin but has not yet found the key to victory over sin. Paul earnestly sought that key from the Lord and was given the great truths of the new covenant, the meaning of which is the Cross.

In brief, the Lord told him that his victory was in the Cross, and with faith there properly placed, the Holy Spirit would then guarantee the victory that had been purchased at such great price (Rom. 8:1-2).

So, the will of man is extremely important, but all it can actually do toward that which is right is cooperate with the Lord. Actually, as far as God is concerned, the will of man is limited to accepting God's way, which is the Cross of Christ, or going in another direction, which the Lord can never honor.

A PERSONAL EXPERIENCE

If I remember correctly, it was 1987. We were in San Jose, Costa Rica, in a crusade. The Lord would move mightily, with many people making the Lord their Saviour in that Central American city. We had been on television there for some time; therefore, the stadium, which seated approximately 50,000 people, was packed to capacity for each service.

We had gone down two or three days early in order to prepare for the meetings. I would spend at least a part of each day seeking the Lord as to His direction for the meetings.

The Lord gave me a dream one night that I think actually referred to two particular things. Let me first relate the dream, and then I will give what I feel the Holy Spirit had given me respecting its meaning.

Swamps are quite common in south Louisiana, actually making up a part of the ecology of the state, as well as the entire southern hemisphere of this great nation.

I dreamed I was in such a swamp, actually, in water a little bit over waist deep. Why I was there, I have no idea.

At any rate, I was wading in the water, moving toward a certain objective, which was a small island. Then I saw a large snake swimming toward me, with me as its objective. It was quite a large serpent, swimming very rapidly, with its head out of the water, coming straight in my direction. This immediately brought fear to my heart, as would be obvious.

THE INVISIBLE SHIELD

I remember my first thought being that I had to somehow get out of the water up on dry ground, which seemed to be about a hundred feet away. After a few moments, I realized that my pace was altogether too slow, and this serpent was going to catch up with me long before I could reach the bank.

In the dream, I watched him come closer and closer, with that ugly head out of the water poised to strike. When it drew within striking distance, only two or three feet from my shoulders and head that were out of the water, I saw him draw back and then lunge toward me, intending to sink those deadly fangs into my arm or shoulder. However, to my surprise, the snake hit something, which seemed to be an invisible shield around me, which I could not see with my eyes, but it definitely was there. The snake's head glanced off. It drew back, made another lunge, and again hit this invisible shield and once again bounced off. This was repeated three or four times, and then it turned and swam away.

I believe the Lord gave me that dream. I personally believe that the meaning is involved in that which I will relate.

I know at least somewhat that of which Paul was speaking when he said, *"And lest I should be exalted above measure through the abundance of the revelations, there was given to me a thorn in the flesh, the messenger of Satan to buffet me, lest I should be exalted above measure"* (II Cor. 12:7).

Unfortunately, I tried to do battle with this thing, so to speak, by what I thought was the Spirit but was actually the flesh. Consequently, such is doomed to failure no matter how strong the struggle. I also know what the great apostle was talking about when he said, *"O wretched man that I am! Who shall deliver me from the body of this death?"* (Rom. 7:24).

THE CROSS

When the Lord did deliver me from that *"body of death,"* He showed me that the way is the Cross, and that when my faith is placed properly in the Cross and not in myself, the Holy Spirit can then do what is needed to be done. When faith is properly placed, it is like the Lord places an unseen shield around the believer that Satan cannot penetrate, exactly as I saw in my dream.

The sadness is that untold millions of Christians at this very moment, and I think I exaggerate not, are struggling exactly as I once did. The Cross has been so little preached in the last few decades that most of the church has been shut off from that which is our only hope and our only victory, for the Lord has provided no other for the simple reason that no other is needed. The Holy Spirit alone can give victory over the flesh, and everything He does is through and by the finished work of Calvary. As stated, we can rest in the finished work, or we can try to finish the work, which is an insult to Christ and is doomed to failure.

The believer must understand that every single soul that's ever been saved, even from the dawn of time, was saved because of what Jesus did at the Cross. Every person who is now in heaven or is on his way there is because of what Jesus did at Calvary. Every believer who has had bondages of darkness broken in his or her life has had them broken because of the Cross. In fact, every single thing the Lord has ever done for us, irrespective of what it is, has been made possible by the Cross of Christ.

WHAT IS THE FLESH AS
PAUL USES THE WORD?

"For the flesh lusteth against the Spirit (Holy Spirit)*, and the Spirit against the flesh: and these are contrary the one to the other: so that you cannot do the things that you would"* (Gal. 5:17).

As Paul uses the word *flesh* again and again, it refers to that which is indicative to a human being. In other words, the flesh is our talent, our education, our motivation, our ability, our willpower, our self-will, etc. In other words, it's that which a human being can do.

The problem is, we cannot live for God, cannot walk victoriously, and cannot be victorious by the means of the flesh. It is impossible. Consequently, the Lord has made a way for victory to be ours, and that way is the Cross, through which the Holy Spirit works.

A characteristic of the contrasts between flesh and Spirit is that the two principles are in deep and irreconcilable conflict. In the sense in which Paul uses the word, the flesh does no good and does not desire good, whereas the Spirit does no evil and indeed opposes anything that does not please the heavenly Father.

Some have maintained that there is no conflict within the Christian because of the supposition that the old nature governed by the flesh has been eradicated, but this is not true according to this and other passages.

Naturally, the flesh is to become increasingly subdued as the Christian learns by grace to walk in the Spirit, but it is never eliminated. It is left for a particular purpose and reason, with which we will deal later.

So, the Christian is never released from the necessity of consciously choosing to go God's way. There is no escape from the need to depend on God's grace, which the Spirit intends, and which demands our faith (ever our faith) in the Cross of Christ.

THE FLESH VERSUS THE HOLY SPIRIT

The phrase, *"For the flesh lusteth against the Spirit, and the Spirit against the flesh,"* could be translated in this manner: "For the flesh constantly has a strong desire to suppress the Holy Spirit, and the Holy Spirit constantly has a strong desire to suppress the flesh. These are entrenched in an attitude of mutual opposition to one another. It means there is war, and no peace will be declared in this conflict" (II Cor. 10:3-5).

When the flesh (in this case, sinful desires) presses hard upon the believer with its evil behests, the Holy Spirit is there to oppose the flesh and give the believer victory over it in order for the believer not to obey the flesh and thus sin. When the Holy Spirit places a course of conduct upon the heart of the believer, the flesh opposes the Spirit in an effort to prevent the believer from obeying the Spirit. The purpose of each is to prevent the believer from doing what the other moves him to do. However, the choice lies with the saint, but only if the faith of the saint is properly placed in the Cross. Otherwise, Satan can override the will of a believer and force him into a course of action he does not desire. Do not misunderstand—the believer has a choice, but it's not a choice as to whether we sin or not. Rather, the choice is whether we obey the Lord by placing our faith exclusively in Christ and the Cross, or if we try to oppose the flesh with the flesh (Rom. 7:15).

Paul uses Galatians 5:17 to substantiate his declaration in the previous verse. The desires of the flesh will not be fulfilled if the believer walks in the Spirit because life in the Spirit is completely opposite to the way of life by the flesh. For the Holy

Spirit to function on our behalf as only He can do, and which He is meant to do, our faith must be exclusively in Christ and the Cross. The Holy Spirit works entirely within the parameters, so to speak, of what Jesus did at the Cross. In other words, it's the Cross of Christ, rather what Jesus there did, that gives the Holy Spirit the legal means to do all that He does with us. He doesn't require much of us, but He does require one thing, and that is that our faith ever be in Christ and the Cross. Otherwise, we tie His hands so to speak (Rom. 6:1-11; I Cor. 1:17-18, 23; 2:2; Rom. 8:1-11; Gal. 6:14; Col. 2:10-15).

Regrettably, the faith of most Christians is not in Christ and the Cross, but rather in themselves.

A PERSONAL EXPERIENCE

The other day, Donnie showed me a book written by a well-known preacher. Please understand that I do not doubt the dear brother's walk with the Lord or his love for Christ, but what he was telling the people was and is wrong.

He was telling the people that if they will fast 21 days, that will give them victory over sin, etc. It won't.

While fasting is definitely scriptural and will definitely be a great blessing to the believer if engaged properly, it will not help one to overcome sin. Such a believer is going to have to eat after awhile, and then the problem will start all over again. What our dear brother didn't realize is that his faith is actually in himself; it's not in Christ and the Cross. Because it's very religious, it deceives us.

That's why Paul also said:

> *For sin* (the sin nature), *taking occasion by the command-
> ment* (the Ten Commandments—in no way blames the
> commandment, but that the commandment actually did
> agitate the sin nature and brought it to the fore, which it
> was designed to do), *deceived me* (Paul thought, now that
> he had accepted Christ, by that mere fact alone, he could
> certainly obey the Lord in every respect; but he found he
> couldn't, and neither can you, at least in that fashion), *and
> by it slew me* (despite all of his efforts to live for the Lord
> by means of law-keeping, he failed; and again I say, so will
> you!) (Rom. 7:11, The Expositor's Study Bible).

In fact, the church, and I mean the church in general, staggers from one fad to the other, all aimless and all worthless. The
Cross and the Cross alone is the solution. It was at the Cross
where all sin was atoned, and Satan and all his cohorts were
roundly defeated (Col. 2:10-15).

AN ERRONEOUS CONCEPT

Too often, Galatians 5:17, taken completely out of context,
is used to teach the two-natured theory, which pictures the
believer as forever torn between two equally powerful forces.
The result is that he lives two lives—serving God with his higher
(or new) nature and serving sin with his lower (or old) nature
(flesh). However, such teaching does serious violence to the

thought of Paul. Most significantly, it ignores the context. Such a view will actually disprove Paul's claim rather than substantiate it. Further, it ignores Paul's clear teaching that the power of the sinful flesh is broken through the Cross. Working from that premise, the flesh, as an instrument of sin, is eradicated. This is what the apostle is teaching. While the flesh itself is not eradicated, as an instrument of sin it definitely is.

That which the Holy Spirit is teaching through the apostle promises victory over all of the power of the carnal nature—a victory that cannot be secured by legal efforts of self-repression. That is something the believer should look at very carefully because this is the great area of conflict—self-repression.

THE SIN NATURE

First of all, let's see what the sin nature actually is: it is that which happened to Adam and Eve at the time of the fall in the garden of Eden. Consequently, every baby that's born is born with a sin nature. Paul tells us how to deal with this thing in Romans 6. Some think it's removed at conversion, but it isn't. In fact, the sin nature will never be removed until we, as believers, die or the trump sounds. Regarding the trump, Paul also said, and we quote again, *"For this corruptible* (sin nature) *must put on incorruption* (a glorified body with no sin nature)*, and this mortal* (subject to death) *must put on immortality* (will never die)" (I Cor. 15:53).

This passage plainly tells us that there is something that is corruptible in every believer, and that corruption is the sin nature. And yet, as stated, Paul tells us how to have victory over the sin nature by the means of the Cross.

At the moment the believing sinner comes to Christ, the sin nature is made dormant. It remains, but it has no power over the new believer. Such a believer thinks in his heart that he'll never sin again, but, eventually, he finds that he does. Now, this is where the problem begins. While the sin itself does not reactivate the sin nature, when the believer places his or her faith in something other than Christ and the Cross, which all do, that is what reactivates the sin nature, and it begins to control the believer.

If the believer doesn't understand the Cross of Christ relative to sanctification, in other words, how we live for God on a daily basis, such a believer is going to be ruled in some way by the sin nature although he or she loves the Lord. Such is a miserable existence. This means that every believer in the world who has his or her faith in something other than Christ and the Cross is at this moment ruled by the sin nature. They don't understand what is happening. They do everything they can to live for God, and they love the Lord supremely; however, they find themselves failing the Lord in some way over and over again.

Let me say it again: If the believer doesn't understand the Cross of Christ relative to how we live for God, such a believer is going to be ruled by the sin nature. This also means that because precious few believers understand the Cross relative to sanctification, the vast majority of believers in the world are being ruled by the sin nature in some way.

PAUL

First of all, it is obvious that Paul's teaching was written to Christians. Paul does not make a habit of calling unsaved people *"brethren"* (Gal. 5:13). So, the reader should not attempt to pull into this scenario the thoughts and actions of a person before he came to Christ. All of this is dealing with a believer, pointing out the struggle, and giving us the key to victory. As it regards the struggle, there are all types of teaching on this particular subject, with most of it being wrong. Let's look at some of the things that are presently taught.

ENTIRE SANCTIFICATION

Some teach entire sanctification, which, of course, leaves these particular passages given by Paul hanging in midair with no explanation. This particular teaching, which is wrong, teaches that a person is saved, and then at a later time, maybe very soon or whenever, he or she is then sanctified. When the person is sanctified, they say the sinful nature is then eradicated, with no more desire in that particular direction. None of this is correct, and such a teaching shows an improper understanding of sanctification.

First of all, every believing sinner is sanctified totally and completely at conversion.

Paul said:

And such were some of you (before conversion): *but you are washed* (refers to the blood of Jesus cleansing from all sin),

> *but you are sanctified* (one's position in Christ), *but you are justified* (declared not guilty) *in the name of the Lord Jesus* (refers to Christ and what He did at the Cross in order that we might be saved), *and by the Spirit of our God* (proclaims the third person of the Triune Godhead as the mechanic, so to speak, in this great work of grace) (I Cor. 6:11, The Expositor's Study Bible).

Justification is being declared clean, but for such to be, one must be made clean, and that is done by being sanctified.

But yet, our *condition* in Christ is not quite up to our *position*. This is the matter of progressive sanctification and where the struggle begins.

The Holy Spirit ever seeks to bring our condition up to our position, but it really cannot be done, at least as it ought to be done, unless the believer places his or her faith exclusively in Christ and the Cross.

THE PHYSICAL BODY

Some teach that after conversion, if sin is committed, it is only the physical body that sins (the flesh) and not the soul and the spirit. They teach that the spirit of man is regenerated and, consequently, cannot sin. Others teach in this same category that when a believer sins, the body and soul sin, but not the spirit. Of course, we are speaking of the spirit of man. However, there is nothing in the Word of God that substantiates such thinking. Actually, the triune make-up of man's spirit, soul, and body is inseparable except at death when the soul and the spirit will then go to be with the Lord, and the physical body will go back to dust. However, when a person is saved, his entire being is saved, and at the same time, when a believer sins, his entire being sins—spirit, soul, and body (I Thess. 5:23).

THE ADAMIC SINFUL NATURE REMOVED?

Some teach that the Adamic sinful nature is removed completely at conversion; however, the apostle Paul taught no such thing. Instead, he taught the necessity of constantly denying the desires of the old sinful nature. On the positive side, he exhorted believers to yield constantly to the new nature of Christ (the divine nature) and to the Holy Spirit, who indwells every believer.

According to Titus 3:5, two basic things happen to a person who accepts Christ. First, God cleanses the individual from sin. Second, the Holy Spirit indwells the person. Jesus taught the same basic thing when He emphasized the absolute necessity of being born of water and of the Spirit in order to enter the kingdom of God (Jn. 3:5).

Romans 8:9 instructs us that if anyone doesn't have the Spirit of Christ, who is the Holy Spirit conferred by Christ, that person does not belong to the Lord; hence, the Holy Spirit indwells every person who has become a Christian.

(However, this which we have just said does not mean that every Christian has been baptized with the Holy Spirit with the evidence of speaking with other tongues, an experience subsequent to salvation that is given for power [Acts 1:8]).

The indwelling Holy Spirit, therefore, is the so-called new nature of Christ that indwells every believer. In a number of places besides Galatians, Paul describes the inward battle that rages within the Christian between the old Adamic nature and the new nature of Christ. For example, in Ephesians 4, he said for us to put off the old man and put on the new man. If the old man is automatically gone at conversion, then what the apostle says makes no sense.

In Romans 6:13, he urges believers not to yield their members as instruments of unrighteousness unto sin, but to yield them unto God as instruments of righteousness. These statements, in addition to many other similar ones in the New Testament, indicate that God does not remove the Adamic nature (sin nature) from a person when that individual is converted to Christ.

THE INNER STRUGGLE

As stated, at conversion God places within the believer a new nature, which is the Holy Spirit. Galatians 2:20 probably gives the clearest account of the inner struggle that rages between the Adamic nature (the sin nature) and the Holy Spirit.

The verb *crucified*, as used in Galatians 2:20 by Paul, indicates an experience that began at the time that Paul was converted and continued unto the very moment that he penned the words. The crucifixion of Paul's Adamic nature began at the time of his salvation experience on the road to Damascus (Acts 9), as it does with every believer. However, at that particular time, immediately after Paul's conversion, according to Romans 7, he did not know how to properly place his faith in Christ and the Cross and, thereby, yield to the Holy Spirit. Consequently, until that great truth was given to him, he lost the battle with the Adamic nature, just as you will, as well, even as he tells us in Romans 7.

However, at a point in time, the Lord gave to Paul the knowledge of how the sin nature works, and how that we have victory over the sin nature by and through the Cross, which is the way that the Holy Spirit works. In other words, Jesus Christ is the new covenant, and the Cross of Christ is the meaning of that new covenant, the meaning of which was given to the apostle Paul, and which he gave to us in his 14 epistles.

Paul learned to place his faith exclusively in Christ, which gave him victory over the sin nature, and which will give you victory over the sin nature also.

Potentially, the power of the sin nature was broken by Christ at Calvary. Legally, it was annulled in the life of the believer at salvation. Experientially, there must be a constant denial of the sin nature and acquiescence to the Holy Spirit, which is done through one's faith in Christ and the Cross. That's the reason that Paul said, *"Christ sent me not to baptize, but to preach the gospel: not with wisdom of words, lest the Cross of Christ should be made of none effect"* (I Cor. 1:17).

Tragically and sadly, the Cross of Christ has been made of none effect in the hearts and lives of most believers.

That's why he also said, *"For I determined not to know anything among you* (with purpose and design, Paul did not resort to the knowledge or philosophy of the world regarding the preaching of the gospel), *save Jesus Christ, and Him crucified* (that and that alone is the message that will save the sinner, set the captive free, and give the believer perpetual victory)*"* (I Cor. 2:2, The Expositor's Study Bible).

INSTRUCTIONS CONCERNING THE HOLY SPIRIT

If one is to notice, Paul does not mention the Cross nearly as much in these statements as he does the Holy Spirit. While he sums up the Cross in Galatians 6:14, which tells us exactly how victory comes for the child of God, still, most of his instruction is given concerning the Holy Spirit.

He does this for a reason. The Cross, and more particularly what Jesus there did, is a fact in history. The only thing the believer has to do is to understand that all of his salvation and victory comes through the Cross, with him ever placing his faith in that finished work. He must understand, as well, that the Cross has to do not only with our salvation, which most understand, but also our daily walk before the Lord, even as we are studying here. Many Christians do not understand that, thinking of the Cross only as it pertains to the born-again experience; however, the Cross has just as much to do with my victory today as it did with my salvation yesterday, in other words, when I came to Christ. The believer must understand that. That's the reason, as we have repeatedly stated, that Jesus commanded us, if you will, to take up the Cross daily and follow Him (Lk. 9:23).

THE WORK OF THE SPIRIT

Once that is done, and I speak of proper faith constantly exhibited in the Cross on a daily basis, that is the extent of the believer's participation in that particular capacity.

However, it is the Holy Spirit who guarantees all of these things done by the Lord at Calvary and the resurrection. To have these great results, which any believer can have and is intended to have, the Holy Spirit must be given latitude in our lives to do His sanctifying work. He is God; consequently, He can do anything that needs to be done. As well, everything He does for us is done through, as stated, the principle of the Cross. That is the sacrifice on which He operates in respect to power exhibited on our behalf.

Learning to cooperate with the Spirit is not altogether easy. That's the reason Paul gave most of his instruction as it regarded this part of the victory process. First of all, the Holy Spirit is a person. Consequently, He is not the same as the act of redemption, which was purchased at Calvary by Christ through the shedding of His precious blood. As we all know, interacting with a person is altogether different than interacting with a principle. A principle is something that is done in which we are to believe, and the results will be ours, at least if it is a valid principle, which the Cross certainly is. However, dealing with a person is something else altogether.

THE PERSON OF THE HOLY SPIRIT

The Holy Spirit is given to us for a particular purpose, and that purpose is not necessarily our purpose, although it certainly ought to be. Consequently, it is His business to bring our desires into His desires, thereby, we depend on Him as He works out the will of God in our lives (Rom. 8:26-27).

It is not that the Holy Spirit is hard to get along with, for He is anything but that. It is just that the Adamic nature (sin nature) that is in all believers does not at all desire His presence and fights against it, with the believer caught in the middle so to speak.

As he anchors his faith in the Cross, the believer learns, little by little, to look to the Spirit, depend on the Spirit, trust in the Spirit, and let the Spirit have His way, which will always bring victorious results.

WHY IS THE SIN NATURE ALLOWED TO REMAIN IN THE BELIEVER?

Man's root problem is pride. In fact, prideful self-will is the result of the fall, which alienates the person from God. This pride shows itself in man by denying what God has said about him, and claiming he is not nearly as bad as the Lord says, that is, if he recognizes God at all. While he (unredeemed man) does admit that there is a problem, he claims that he can solve that problem by his own machinations. Consequently, the struggle is between the prideful self-will of man, which institutes and proposes his own self-righteousness, versus God's imputed righteousness.

Even after coming to Christ, pride continues to be the root cause in one way or the other of all problems. It's like Israel and the law.

God gave Israel the law, demanded that they keep the law, and foretold a serious penalty for their failure to not obey its commands, but He gave no power to carry out this task, even though He knew that man could not do what was required. On the surface, such seems to be cruel; however, it is the very opposite. It is actually mercy on the part of God.

If God had given man the power and ability to keep the law, it would not have fallen out to obedience of the heart, but rather to pride. In other words, power to obey, at least in that capacity, would have only tended toward pride and not humility. The Christian has the same problem.

In order for the Christian to be made humble and to remain humble, in fact, to be broken before the Lord, in which Christ can then be correctly portrayed, there must be some factor within man that will keep him dependent on the Lord. Of course, I am speaking of believing man. It is the same struggle, irrespective of the sign on the door—the struggle between self and the Spirit of God.

HUMILITY

So, the Lord leaves the sinful nature in man after he is converted, which, of course, is an ever-present danger.

After failing a few times, even many times, and now realizing the danger involved, the idea is for the believer to learn that even though he is saved, actually, a new creation in Christ Jesus, still, he must have the help of the Holy Spirit to do what he needs to do and live as he needs to live. Inasmuch as the sin nature is a constant threat, such demands a constant dependence on the Lord, which is the intention all along. This dependence opposes pride and brings about humility (Isa. 66:2).

Even the knowledge that one cannot attain to victory on his own, and must have the help of the Holy Spirit on a constant basis, still is not quite enough to address this monster called pride. It should be enough, but the results of the fall are so ever evident that this danger is far more acute than most of us realize.

Hence, the Lord at times allows very difficult situations to develop, even as He did with the apostle Paul, *"Lest I should be exalted above measure"* (II Cor. 12:7).

The only thing that Jesus ever said about Himself personally was, *"I am meek and lowly in heart"* (Mat. 11:29). He, as always, is our example; however, because of the reasons mentioned, that example cannot be reached within our hearts and lives without a constant dependence upon the Holy Spirit, with at times even more stringent measures thrown in. In other words, the sin nature is allowed to remain in us for disciplinary reasons.

HOW BIG OF A PROBLEM IS THE SIN NATURE?

In truth, the sin nature, or Adamic nature as it is sometimes called, is not really the problem. The moment the believer comes to Christ, even though the Lord allows the sin nature to remain, it is no longer active, or at least it's not supposed to be.

Before conversion, the sin nature dominated the person. After conversion, *"sin* (the sin nature) *shall not have dominion over you: for you are not under the law, but under grace"* (Rom. 6:14). Even though present, it is actually dormant in the believer until …

Until what? It is until the believer fails the Lord, in other words, sins. Such causes great consternation for the new believer, even as it should, and this is where the problem begins.

Such a believer—and I believe that all of us have fallen into that category—now determines never to fail again. To bring this about, we place our faith in something other than Christ and the Cross, which always fails. It's the natural thing to do, or so it seems. When we place our faith in the wrong object, which means anything other than Christ and the Cross, then the sin nature springs to life and begins to cause us great problems.

Actually, the sin nature is not really the origin of sin in the believer, with such only pertaining to the fuel for the fire so to speak. Sin originates in the heart of man, so that means it is not permissible to blame our failure on outside forces or even on a particular direction, which is the sin nature. In other words, that nature is the very opposite of God, which was brought about at the fall. As far as sin per se is concerned, as previously stated, such originates in the heart of man. That's why Jesus said, *"For out of the heart proceed evil thoughts, murders, adulteries, fornications, thefts, false witness, blasphemies"* (Mat. 15:19).

That means we cannot blame our problem on the sin nature or even other particulars, but rather ourselves.

WHAT IS THE BELIEVER TO DO?

No Christian needs to fail the Lord; however, due to these problems that we are discussing, every single Christian has failed the Lord, and many times for that matter. It grieves the heart to have to say and admit that, but it is true.

As stated, when this happens, as we put our faith in something other than Christ and the Cross, the sin nature then springs to life. It's not actually sin that causes such to be, but rather the wrong object of our faith. The sin is the fuel that brings it to life, and the sin nature itself then burns the fuel. Satan, through the sin nature, wants to dominate the Christian, which he does in many cases. Now you have a believer who is serving the Lord, or at least trying to, and at the same time, obeying evil impulses.

The reason that the sin nature gains the upper hand in many Christians, with the sin nature then dominating the believer, is because the believer tries to overcome the thing within his own strength, even though most of the time he thinks he is doing so by the help of the Lord.

The believer should understand why he failed to start with. Many answers may be given in regard to this, but the real reason is that he is not properly looking toward the Cross and understanding that he has victory in that which Jesus did, and that alone. In other words, the Cross of Christ is the only source of victory, and I mean the *only* source. However, many, sad to say, don't understand that.

Failure in a Christian should not be to begin with, but it always has been in every Christian in one way or the other.

Upon the advent of failure, the believer must renew his faith in what Christ did at Calvary. He must claim that victory as his own, and the Holy Spirit will then exhibit the power needed for failure not to occur again, at least as a dominating factor. While the Bible does not teach sinless perfection, it most definitely does teach that sin is not to have dominion over us (Rom. 6:14). That's where the saint wants to be, and that's where the Holy Spirit desires that we be, and He works toward that end constantly.

As we anchor our faith in the Cross, with the Holy Spirit guaranteeing our victory, the sin nature once again becomes dormant and is no more a problem to the believer.

As we have stated, if one is to notice, Paul nowhere teaches sinless perfection, but he does teach, as also stated, that sin is not to have dominion over us—ever.

The subjection of the saint to the personal control of the indwelling Holy Spirit, which is derived through our faith in the Cross, is the secret of victory over sin and of living a life in which divine love is the motivating impulse (Gal. 5:16-26).

As well, if our faith is in Christ and the Cross, the Holy Spirit will suppress the activities of the evil nature as the saint trusts Him to do so and cooperates with Him in His work of sanctification (Gal. 5:16-21).

CONTRARY

The phrase, *"And these are contrary the one to the other,"* refers to the flesh and the Holy Spirit and their obvious antagonism. In fact, they can never harmonize.

As an Old Testament type, we are given the account of the battle between Moses and Amalek not long after Israel left Egypt and came into the wilderness.

Immediately before Amalek, the account is given of the smiting of the rock, which is a type of Jesus being smitten at Calvary, with the water coming out, which was a type of the Holy Spirit (Ex. 17:5-6).

The water from the smitten rock—Christ—foretold the Living Water—the Holy Spirit—to be sent forth by the smitten Saviour. The Holy Spirit was shed forth as the fruit of Christ's sacrifice (I Cor. 10:4). The rock was smitten by the very same rod of judgment that smote the land of Egypt.

The reception of the Holy Spirit immediately causes war. *"Then came Amalek, and fought with Israel"* (Ex. 17:8-16).

Up to this point, God had fought for them. Israel was to stand still and see His salvation, but the command now was to go out and fight. There is an immense difference between justification and sanctification, which we are studying here.

The one is Christ fighting for us; the other is the Holy Spirit fighting in us. The entrance of the new nature is the beginning of warfare with the old.

AMALEK

Williams said:

Amalek pictures the old carnal nature. He was the grandson of Esau, who before and after birth tried to murder Jacob, and who preferred the mess of pottage to the birthright. This carnal nature wars against the Spirit, 'it is not subject to the law of God, neither indeed can be,' and God has decreed war against it forever. The victory over Amalek hung upon the intercession of Moses, and upon the wisdom and valor of Joshua. Christ is both Moses and Joshua to His people – excepting that His hands never grow weary.

God did not destroy Amalek, which was a type of the flesh, but determined to have war with him from generation to generation. Amalek was to dwell in the land but not to reign in it. Romans 6:12 says, *"Let not sin* (the sin nature) *therefore reign in your mortal body."* This command would be without meaning if the sin nature were not existent in the Christian. Sin dwells in a believer, but dwells and reigns in an unbeliever. Whenever the trump sounds and this corruptible puts on incorruption, and this mortal puts on immortality, then sin, or even the potential of such, will no longer dwell in any capacity in the Christian (I Cor. 15:53-54).

THE POWERFUL FORCE OF SIN

It is sad that the world does not know or understand the terrible power of sin, even though it is wreaking havoc all around them constantly. Sadder still is the fact that the church, at least for the most part, doesn't understand the potency of sin either. How do I know that?

First, sin is so powerful that God could not speak redemption into existence and be true to His nature. He could speak the worlds into existence, and all of creation for that matter (Gen. 1; Heb. 11:3), but could not bring about redemption by the spoken word. God had to become man and pay the supreme price by dying on a Cross in order for man to be saved. In viewing the situation in this manner, I think it becomes obvious how deadly, how awful, and how powerful that sin really is. In fact, it is so powerful that the Cross alone can address this monster, and that's where the church makes its mistake. It embraces humanistic psychology and all such like efforts, all to no avail. Let us say it again: it is the Cross and the Cross alone that is the solution for sin.

If the church understood this, they would hardly recommend humanistic psychology as the answer to the terrible problems of humanity. The ridiculous statement of the church, "You need professional help," is an admittance that they have forsaken the ways of the Lord, *"And hewed them out cisterns, broken cisterns, that can hold no water"* (Jer. 2:13).

If a psychologist can cure man of his sinful nature, his aberrations, or his personality quirks, then Jesus did not need to come down here and die on Calvary. That should be obvious!

THE LIMITATION OF THE PERSONAL
ABILITY OF BELIEVERS

The phrase, *"So that you cannot do the things that you would,"* could be translated "so that you do not what you would." The original Greek actually means that there is no possibility of the impossibility and no ability of the inability. It is a statement of fact (Rom. 7:15, 19). As is obvious, Paul is speaking of the personal ability of the believer, which means without the help of the Holy Spirit.

The idea is that without the help of the Holy Spirit, there is no way that we can be what we ought to be in Christ. It is just that simple; however, please notice what He said: *"You cannot do"* and not "God cannot do," for the Lord most definitely can do!

So, this phrase emphatically states that without the Holy Spirit helping us, there is no way that we can overcome Satan, overcome sin, or do what we ought to do, no matter how much willpower we may have, and no matter how much desire we may have. Such simply does not lie within the personal strength or ability of the believer. And yet, most of the so-called Christian world is trying to do these things, which we know we must do, without the Holy Spirit. Taking that route, we are shot down before we even begin.

THE BELIEVER AND THE HOLY SPIRIT

Forgive the repetition, but due to the seriousness of this matter and how much it affects the believer, I'm hoping you can read it enough until finally it will begin to click in your spirit, at least if it has not already done so.

The work of the Holy Spirit in the life of the believer is not an automatic thing. The potential is there, but potential only. Realizing that potential is predicated on many things. I will not take the time to go into all the particulars, but I will deal with the most important as it addresses itself to this particular problem.

When we speak of the help of the Holy Spirit, most Christians think that He automatically steps in and takes care of the problem, whatever the problem is. Of course, I'm speaking of those who believe in what we are saying and not the myriad of Christians who little believe in the Holy Spirit or His working or power. For them, to be frank, there is little hope at all.

COOPERATION

The Holy Spirit must have cooperation. That means that we understand that He lives within our hearts and lives, and that He is there for a purpose. Among other things, that purpose is to maintain our victory.

We are to exhibit faith in Christ and the Cross, understanding that all blessings, all help, all healing, all salvation, and all deliverance come through the Cross. When we exhibit faith accordingly, believing that the price was there paid and the victory was won by Christ, the Holy Spirit will then give us His power, and the problem will be solved without any difficulty.

To be sure, Satan will test your faith, with the Lord allowing him to do so (Lk. 22:31-32). Because he does that, with the problem (whatever it is) seemingly at times getting worse, many believers quit and transfer their hopes elsewhere. That's the road to disaster. You are to believe and not stop believing. Even if in the midst of this believing you fail, ask the Lord to forgive you and get back up and start all over again. Don't quit believing, and victory is guaranteed. Of course, we're speaking of believing in Christ and what He did for us at the Cross.

Satan will test our faith to see whether we mean business or not, and, as stated, the Lord will allow him certain latitude. As someone has said, "All faith must be tested, and great faith must be tested greatly."

MORE ABOUT THE HOLY SPIRIT

"But if you be led of the Spirit, you are not under the law" (Gal. 5:18).

The final verse of the section is best taken as a summary in which Paul reminds the Galatians that, though he is not talking about the absolute necessity of living a godly life, he is not, thereby, reverting to legalism. Life by the Spirit is neither legalism nor license, nor a middle way between them. It is a life of faith and love that is above all of these false ways.

Being led by the Holy Spirit does not imply passivity, even as we have just attempted to describe, but rather the need to allow oneself to be led. Responding to the Spirit is described by three mutually interpreting words in verses 16, 18, and 25: walk, led, and live.

That the Holy Spirit and the flesh are now in conflict is illustrated by contrasting lists of the works of the flesh and the fruit of the Spirit. Paul has both in mind as he begins to write this section. At the same time, the lists are more than a mere proof of what he has written earlier, for by raising these particulars of conduct, he also provides a checklist for measuring the conduct of those who consider themselves spiritual. If one's conduct is characterized by the traits in the first list, then he is either not a believer, or else, a believer who is not being led by the Holy Spirit. The same standards of evaluation hold true for churches.

THE HOLY SPIRIT

The phrase, *"But if you be led of the Spirit,"* tells us by the use of the word *if* that it is possible, as should be obvious, for the saint to not be led by the Spirit. The idea is that one cannot be led by the Spirit and be under the law at the same time, and anything that is not Christ and Him crucified is law. While it may not be law within itself, when we place our faith in such, whatever it might be, it then becomes law.

The expression, *"led of the Spirit"* is parallel to *"walk in the Spirit."* However, the term *led* emphasizes the submission of the believer to the Holy Spirit. Up to the time of the Judaizers' entry into their churches, the Galatian Christians had lived their Christian lives in dependence upon the Holy Spirit in accordance with the teaching of the apostle Paul. The power of the sinful nature had been broken, the divine nature had been implanted, and the Spirit had entered their hearts to take up His permanent residence.

While there had been conflict in their lives exactly as it is in all believers, which is spoken of in verse 17, the result had been that they were living victorious lives over sin.

However, now a new factor had entered—the law—and with it, their dependence upon self-effort to obey that law. While the Galatians were still trying to live Christian lives, they were going about it in the wrong way, with the result that they were failing. The entrance of these new factors meant that the Spirit had no opportunity to minister to their spiritual lives. The mechanical setup of spiritual machinery that God had installed had become ineffective by reason of the monkey wrench of self-dependence that the Galatians had thrown into it as a result of now depending upon law.

WAYS OPEN TO THE BELIEVER

The believer can attempt to function under law, meaning to live an overcoming life by this particular route, which, in fact, characterizes most of the church. While it is not the law of Moses that modern believers attempt to keep, it is still a law, but rather that of their own making or the making of someone else. This can go in many directions, actually, any direction other than that of the Holy Spirit.

Most of the laws we make up are borrowed and are all spiritual in one way or the other, and because they are spiritual, it deceives us into thinking it is the Holy Spirit when it isn't.

For instance, there are untold numbers of churches in the land that draw up a system of laws to which believers must subscribe, that is, if they are to belong to that particular church. To be frank, the laws probably are good, and my statements are not meant to disparage that for which they seek; however, these rules and regulations of churches will not attain the intended result, which is to keep people above sin, but rather the very opposite, which is characteristic of all law. Maybe it's not laws instituted by our church, but rather those of our own making. It really doesn't matter; there is no victory whatsoever from this source.

NO RESTRAINTS?

Many have gone the exact opposite and abandoned the restraints of any type of law, for the simple reason that they don't work anyway. Not having the power of the Holy Spirit, they are left without restraint of any kind and, thus, yield to the impulses of the evil nature. These individuals generally operate under the premise that grace covers all sin; therefore, they make no effort to rid themselves of this monster. Having tried and failed, possibly even many times, they now yield to ungodly passions, which, of course, is a road to ruin.

The right way is not a middle road between these two (law or no law) but a highway above them. It is a highway of freedom from statutes and from the sinful nature. It is a highway that is a faith way, a dependence upon the Holy Spirit, which actually refers to a dependence on Christ and the Cross.

The exhortation is, therefore, to be led by the Spirit. The assurance is given to those who do so that they will not be living their lives on the principle of legalism. The man led by the Spirit can now do what he desires to do, which is to have the will of God carried out within his life.

NOT UNDER THE LAW

The phrase, *"You are not under the law,"* proclaims the fact that the believer will find no victory by this method. The law is not only no safeguard against the flesh, but rather provokes it to more sin. Therefore, the believer who would renounce the flesh must also renounce the law. Thus, the flesh and the law are closely allied, whereas the flesh and the Spirit are diametrically opposed to one another.

In fact, the law finds nothing to condemn in the life of the person who is led by the Spirit, for that person checks every wrong desire that is brought to him by the evil nature, and so he fulfills the law. This is the blessed moral freedom of the person who is led by the Holy Spirit. He is in such a condition of moral and spiritual life that the law has no power to censure, condemn, or punish him. This is the true moral freedom from the law to which Paul refers when he says, *"There is therefore now no condemnation to them which are in Christ Jesus, who walk not after the flesh, but after the Spirit"* (Rom. 8:1).

THE FLESH AND THE LAW

The flesh and the law are correlative terms—to be free from the one is to be free from the other.

The flesh represents unaided human nature, and law is the standard to which this unaided human nature thrives, but thrives in vain to fulfill.

By the intervention of the Holy Spirit, the law is fulfilled at the same time that its domination is abolished, and human nature ceases to be unaided. In other words, it is now aided by the Holy Spirit.

In its highest part, human nature is now brought into direct contact with the divine nature, and the whole tenor of its actions changes accordingly. Now, the reader must understand that we can walk after the Spirit, or we might say "live in the Spirit," only by placing our faith exclusively in Christ and what Christ has done for us at the Cross. The Cross is that through which the Holy Spirit works. Of course, we are speaking of what Jesus there did (what He accomplished) and did so by atoning for all sin. In fact, we cannot have the working and the operation of the Holy Spirit within our lives, helping us to overcome sin and shame, unless our faith is planted directly in the Cross of Christ.

The baptism with the Holy Spirit is given to the child of God to help him in his service for the Lord. It will help the preacher to preach, the layperson to witness, etc. However, it must be understood that the baptism with the Holy Spirit with the evidence of speaking with other tongues is strictly for service, and while He most definitely will help us in every way, still, His role is not exactly to give us victory over sin. While He most definitely will do that, which we will explain in a moment, that comes in another way.

The moment the believing sinner comes to Christ, the Holy Spirit comes into that heart and life. In fact, a person cannot be saved without the regenerating power of the Holy Spirit. However, that is totally different than the baptism with the Holy Spirit with the evidence of speaking with other tongues. We might say it this way: there is a great difference in being born of the Spirit and being baptized with the Spirit.

When Jesus addressed His followers just before His ascension, He told them to go to Jerusalem and wait for the promise of the Father (Acts 1:1-4). This they did and turned the world of that day upside down.

Millions have been baptized with the Holy Spirit, which every believer most definitely ought to receive, and still are not able to live a victorious life in their own living.

Now, let's say that again: if the believer doesn't understand the Cross of Christ relative to sanctification and how the Holy Spirit works in that capacity, while he may be used of God, and used greatly, still, he will not be able to live a victorious life regarding his personal living.

Paul addressed this very thing by saying, *"For I know that in me (that is, in my flesh,) dwells no good thing: for to will is present with me; but how to perform that which is good I find not. For the good that I would I do not: but the evil which I would not, that I do"* (Rom. 7:18-19).

Whenever Paul was undergoing this situation, he was saved, baptized with the Holy Spirit, and preaching the gospel. Actually, at this time, he was an apostle, and yet he still did not know how to have victory in his own life.

In Paul's defense, this great revelation had not yet been given, and, of course, we are speaking of the revelation of the new covenant, the meaning of which is the Cross. In fact, that great revelation would be given to the apostle Paul, which he gave to us in his 14 epistles.

VICTORY OVER SIN

To have victory over sin, which is a must for any and every believer, such a believer must place his or her faith exclusively in Christ and the Cross.

Notice again what Paul said: *"For the preaching of the Cross is to them who perish foolishness; but unto us who are saved it is the power of God"* (I Cor. 1:18).

The word *power*, as used in this verse, is the same as the word *power* in the following verse: *"But you shall receive power, after that the Holy Spirit is come upon you: and you shall be witnesses unto Me"* (Acts 1:8).

However, this power just quoted is for service. The power quoted by Paul in I Corinthians 1:18 is power to live a holy life. They are two different things.

Perhaps we could say it this way: To live an overcoming life, which necessitates us having the power of the Holy Spirit, our faith must be in Christ and the Cross, and Christ and the Cross exclusively. When that is done, the Holy Spirit, who works exclusively by and through the Cross of Christ, will then work mightily within our lives, helping us to be what we ought to be.

That's what Paul also was mentioning when he said: *"There is therefore now no condemnation to them which are in Christ Jesus, who walk not after the flesh, but after the Spirit."*

He then said, *"For the law of the Spirit of life in Christ Jesus has made me free from the law of sin and death"* (Rom. 8:1-2).

In the advent light, Oh Saviour,
I am living day by day;
Waiting, working, watching ever,
Knowing Thou are on Thy way.

Separated unto Jesus,
Loosed from all the world beside;
Blinded by the advent glory,
Hour by hour would I abide.

So from glory unto glory,
Gladdened by the advent ray;
All the path is growing brighter,
Shining unto perfect day.

In the Advent Light to witness,
To a dark and dying world;
This the holy ordination;
May His banner be unfurled.

In the Advent Light rejoicing;
Songs of praise along the road,
Seem to make the journey shorter,
Mounting upward to our God.

He is coming! He is coming!
Pass the heavenly watchword on:
Go ye forth to meet the Bridegroom,
Hail! To God's anointed Son."

See the advent glory breaking;
Faith will soon be lost in sight,
Face to face I shall behold Him,
Bathed in His eternal light.

THE YOKE OF BONDAGE

CHAPTER 6

WORKS OF THE FLESH

WORKS OF THE FLESH

"NOW THE WORKS OF the flesh are manifest, which are these; Adultery, fornication, uncleanness, lasciviousness" (Gal. 5:19).

LIVING OUTSIDE OF THE CROSS

When Paul says that the acts of the flesh are obvious, he does not mean that they are all committed publicly where they may be seen. Some are, but some are not. Instead, he means that it is obvious to all that such acts originate with the sinful nature and not with the nature given believers by God. Here the full scope of the word *flesh* becomes evident (if it was not so before), for the list does not contain only the so-called fleshly sins. It contains sins that emanate from every part of human nature.

It is impossible to tell whether Paul was thinking in categories of sin as he wrote. Whether or not he did, four divisions in his list are obvious:

1. Four sins that are violations of sexual morality;
2. Two sins from the religious realm;

3. Nine sins pertaining to conduct in regard to other human beings—social sins; and
4. Two typically pagan sins accompanying it: drunkenness and reveling.

WORKS OF THE FLESH

The phrase, *"Now the works of the flesh are manifest, which are these,"* presents the apostle presenting a catalog of sins that are repulsive to the true believer. It is as if Paul is saying to the Galatians, "You have a clearly defined standard by which to decide whether you are being led by the Holy Spirit or by the flesh. Each is known by its peculiar works or fruits."

The word *manifest* in the Greek is *phaneros* and means "open, evident." The idea is that if the believer resorts to the law, some part of these sins are going to be manifested in such a person, despite his efforts otherwise.

As well, if a believer does not avail himself of the help given by the Holy Spirit, consequently, resorting to law, ultimately, even as the latter portion of verse 21 tells us, that person can lose his soul. This is what Paul is speaking of in Galatians 5:4. Such an individual has shifted his faith from the Cross to law. This is certain for the simple reason that all began at the Cross, for that is the only way one can be saved. In fact, the thrust of this epistle to the Galatians is that it is a sure road to disaster for the believer who begins in the Spirit (by means of the Cross) and then reverts to law (works) as it regards his everyday walk before God.

Without being very precise, the works of the flesh fall into four general sections: sensuality, idolatry, contention, and excess.

ACTS AND ACTIONS

Due to the fact that we're looking at the acts and actions of believers, I think it would be profitable to do a little more investigation, not only as it regards human beings but, also, as it regards God.

Both human beings and God are portrayed in the Bible as persons who act freely and responsibly in the material universe.

For the entirety of the epistle to the Galatians, Paul has been addressing himself to the reason that acts of ill nature are performed, in other words, sin! However, all actions, whether they are good or bad, should be looked at from the biblical perspective and, in fact, must be looked at from that perspective.

THE OLD TESTAMENT

In passages where the Hebrew terms have moral or spiritual significance, the King James Bible usually renders these terms as either "doings" or "deeds." Some of the other versions sometimes have "deeds" but more frequently use "acts" or "actions."

The most common Hebrew word that expresses the idea of acts or actions is *asah,* which means "to do, to fashion, or to accomplish." When this word is used of God, it emphasizes His acts in history. God is not distant or removed from the physical universe He created. God is fully able to act in the material world.

The Hebrew word *ma-sch* is translated as "actions or deeds" and is often applied to the awesome works that God has performed (Ps. 66:3; 118:17).

Presently, other Hebrew words related to the verb *alal* are also rendered as deeds or actions. When used of human actions, these words have a strong negative connotation and emphasize the wicked quality of particular actions. In contrast, when God is the subject, the same words stress the righteous quality of His actions (Ps. 66:5; 105:1).

THE MORAL FRAMEWORK
OF HUMAN ACTIONS

Human actions are not morally neutral. They are responsible for our choices, and responsibility is reflected in many Old Testament descriptive terms. The Old Testament decries the fact that people at times act:

- Deceitfully (Ex. 8:29)
- Impurely (Lev. 20:21)
- Treacherously (Judg. 9:23)
- Irreverently (II Sam. 6:7)
- Wickedly (II Chron. 6:37)
- Corruptly (Jer. 6:28; Zech. 3:7)
- Lewdly (Ezek. 22:9)

The prophets Jeremiah and Ezekiel were particularly critical of the immoral conduct and actions of the people of Judah just prior to the Babylonian captivity (Jer. 4:18; 7:3, 5; 18:11; 26:13; 35:15; Ezek. 14:22-23; 24:14; 36:17, 19).

The Old Testament establishes the standard by which human actions can be judged. All Israel was called to act in accordance with what *"is written in the law in the book of Moses"* (II Chron. 25:4). Therefore, righteous and honest actions can be known, and *"every prudent man"* can act on this knowledge (Judg. 9:16, 19; I Sam. 12:7; II Ki. 12:15; Prov. 13:16).

By comparing actions of the individual with the moral framework provided in the divine law, even a child is known by his actions (Prov. 20:11). As Micah 6:8 reminded an indifferent generation, *"He has shown you, O man, what is good; and what does the LORD require of you, but to do* (to act) *justly, and to love mercy, and to walk humbly with your God."*

God hates the vile deeds of the corrupt (Ps. 14:1). He has provided a revelation of the moral framework within which human beings are to choose to live.

GOD'S MIGHTY ACTS IN HISTORY

The descriptive words linked with God's actions tend to stress His greatness and His power. God's deeds are mighty (Ps. 71:16; 106:2; 145:4, 12), awesome (Ps. 65:5; 66:3), wonderful (Ps. 26:7; 105:2), and marvelous (Ps. 71:17; 72:18; 86:10). They are acts of power (Ps. 150:2). His acts are also righteous (Ps. 71:24) and praiseworthy (Ps. 78:4).

An awed sense of wonder at God's ability to act in history grips the writers of the Old Testament. "Has any god ever tried to take for Himself one nation out of another nation," Moses asked, "by testings, by miraculous signs and wonders, by war, by a mighty hand and an out-stretched arm, or by great and awesome deeds, like all the things the Lord your God did for you in Egypt before your very eyes?" (Deut. 4:34).

The God of the Old Testament is a God with unlimited ability to act in the world of human beings. Confident of this fact, Jonathan and a single armorbearer boldly attacked a detachment of Philistines (I Sam. 14:6, 13). Similarly, God's Old Testament saints cried out in prayer, "It is time for You to act, Oh Lord" (Ps. 119:126; Dan. 9:19).

God's acts in creation in bringing the Genesis flood and in redeeming Israel from Egypt are to be told and retold by His people (I Chron. 16:9), so that His people will stand in awe of the Lord and of His deeds (Hab. 3:2). Our concept of what God is like ought to be shaped by the conviction that He lives, and He is able to act on our behalf.

THE NEW TESTAMENT

New Testament Greek words that are usually translated as "doings," "deeds" and "works" are sometimes rendered as "acts" and "actions."

The New Testament makes clear that lawless deeds erupt from man's sinful nature, even as we are now studying (Gal. 5:19-21).

However, there is no doubt that the New Testament emphasis is on good deeds and actions—an appropriate emphasis for a believing community who professes to worship God (I Tim. 2:10; 5:10; 6:18; Heb. 10:24).

While the Old Testament directed our attention to external standards by which one could assess the good or evil character of one's actions, the New Testament, quite the contrary, directs our attention within—to the source of goodness or evil.

It is the Cross of Christ that made this possible. At the moment the believing sinner comes to Christ, the Holy Spirit comes in to such a believer and is there to perform a task. That task is to bring our spiritual condition up to our spiritual position. The moment a person comes to Christ, he is instantly and fully sanctified.

In the book of I Corinthians, Paul lists a long catalog of various different sins and sinners. He then says, *"And such were some of you* (before conversion)*: but you are washed* (refers to the blood of Jesus cleansing from all sin)*, but you are sanctified* (one's position in Christ)*, but you are justified* (declared not guilty) *in the name of the Lord Jesus* (refers to Christ and what He did at the Cross in order that we might be saved)*, and by the Spirit of our God* (proclaims the third person of the triune Godhead as the mechanic in this great work of grace)*"* (I Cor. 6:9-11, The Expositor's Study Bible).

That which we have listed is positional sanctification—one's position in Christ—which automatically comes at conversion. Now we come to progressive sanctification, which is the Holy Spirit endeavoring to bring our condition up to our position. That's what Paul was talking about in I Thessalonians 5:23. I'll quote from The Expositor's Study Bible:

And the very God of peace sanctify you wholly (this is 'progressive sanctification,' which can only be brought about by the Holy Spirit, who does such as our faith is firmly anchored in the Cross, within which parameters the Spirit always works; the sanctification process is an ongoing factor in the life of the believer, and involves the whole man); *and I pray God your whole spirit and soul and body* (proclaims the make-up of the whole man) *be preserved blameless unto the coming of our Lord Jesus Christ.* (This refers to the rapture. As well, this one verse proclaims the fact that any involvement, whether righteous or unrighteous, affects the whole man, and not just the physical body or the soul as some claim).

We find that Paul's teaching is that the Holy Spirit works conclusively within the parameters of the Cross of Christ. This means that what Jesus did at the Cross is what gives the Holy Spirit the legal means to do all that He does for us and with us (Rom. 8:2).

For us to have the help of the Holy Spirit, which we must have, and which He readily gives, He demands that our faith be exclusively in Christ and what Christ has done for us at the Cross (I Cor. 1:17, 18; 2:2).

With our faith maintained in Christ and the Cross, the Holy Spirit will then work mightily on our behalf, giving us victory over the world, the flesh, and the Devil. To be sure, this is God's way of life and living—His way of victory. He has no other because no other is needed.

THE CROSS

That's why Jesus came to this world, in other words, God became man— the incarnation. While everything He did was of vast significance, still, the Cross was His main objective. That's the reason He came. God demanded full payment for the sin that man had committed against Him, and to be sure, man could not pay that debt. So, if it was to be paid, God would have to pay it Himself.

As well, He could not shortcut the situation, for that would be in opposition to His nature of pure holiness. So, the price would have to be paid in totality, which was done at Calvary's Cross. The price demanded was the shedding of perfect, spotless blood, which atoned for all sin—past, present, and future—at least for all who will believe.

All of this means that the Cross of Christ is the solution, and the only solution, for man's dilemma. This is the reason the world constantly strikes out when they try to deal with the forces of evil of man's concoctions. It simply cannot be done. As well, that's where the church goes wrong when it ignores the Cross and, thereby, inserts something else to take its place. There is nothing else that can take its place. It's the Cross, the Cross, *the Cross*!

The following proclaims a list as given by the apostle Paul of that which is labeled *"the works of the flesh."* Unless the believer's faith is exclusively in Christ and the Cross, sooner or later one or more of these evil works is going to manifest itself in such a life. In other words, such a person will be ruled by the sin nature.

That's what Paul is relating to his readers. Please understand that what was the case then is the case now.

The only way the believer can throttle the sin nature, in other words, make it dormant or ineffective within his life, is for his faith to be exclusively in Christ and the Cross. If his faith is in anything else, there will be a revival of the sin nature, which will rule the believer, no matter how hard he tries to live right otherwise. In other words, he simply won't be able to do what he knows he needs to do. God's way is the Cross, and as we have repeatedly stated, it is the only way. When we study the following, it's not a pretty picture, so we need to consider all things carefully. We can go God's way, which is the Cross, or we can go the way of the flesh, i.e., works. The latter will lead to wreckage and ruin. The former will lead to victory. Now let's look at this list.

ADULTERY

The first four works related by Paul address sexual gratification and suggest gross depravity. Paul begins here because of the moral climate of the world in which he lived. Every imaginable form of immorality in those days was commonly and openly practiced by rulers, aristocracy, philosophers, poets, priests, and worshippers—with no sense of shame or remorse. In those days, it was the accepted way of life, and it is pretty much the same presently.

It is little wonder that this is a problem with which Paul greatly concerned himself as he dealt with his converts from paganism. He would countenance no compromise; immorality could have no place in the Christian life.

The word *adultery* in the Greek is moicheia and means "unlawful sexual relations between men and women, single or married" (but not married to each other). This term is not used in the broader sense of all forms of unchastity as in fornication. In a sense, all fornication is adultery, but all adultery is not fornication.

FORNICATION

The word *fornication* in the Greek is porneia and means "repeated adultery of married or single people" (Mat. 5:32; 19:9; I Cor. 7:2; 10:8; I Thess. 4:3; Rev. 9:21); incest (I Cor. 5:1; 10:8); idolatry and adultery in honor of idol gods (II Chron. 21:11; Isa. 23:17; Ezek. 16:15, 26, 29; Acts 15:20, 29; 21:25; Rev. 2:14-21; 14:8; 17:2-4; 18:3-9; 19:2); natural harlotry (Jn. 8:41; I Cor. 6:13-18); and spiritual harlotry (Ezek. 16:15, 26, 29; Rev. 17:2-4; 18:3-9; 19:2). Whenever a believer places his or her faith in something other than Christ and the Cross, no matter how religious the other thing may be, in the eyes of God, such a person is committing spiritual harlotry (Rom. 7:1-4; II Cor. 11:1-4); sodomy and male prostitution (Rom. 1:24-29; I Cor. 6:9-11; II Cor. 12:21; Gal. 5:19; Eph. 5:3; Col. 3:5; Heb. 12:16; Jude, Vss. 6-7).

Do all of these Scriptures apply to single people only? If not, then fornication does not apply only to single people as some teach, with adultery applying only to married people.

UNCLEANLINESS

The word *uncleanliness* in the Greek is akatharsia and refers to "whatever is opposite of purity," including sodomy, homosexuality, lesbianism, pederasty, bestiality, and all other forms of sexual perversions (Mat. 12:27; Rom. 1:21-32; 6:19; II Cor. 12:21; Eph. 4:19; 5:3; Col. 3:5; I Thess. 2:3; 4:7; II Pet., Chpt. 2; Jude)

LASCIVIOUSNESS

The word *lasciviousness* in the Greek is aselgeia and means "lustfulness, unchastity, and lewdness" (Mk. 7:22; II Cor. 12:21; Gal. 5:19; Eph. 4:19; I Pet. 4:3; Jude, Vs. 4); it also means "wantonness" (Rom. 13:13; II Pet. 2:18); and "filthy" (II Pet. 2:7).

Lasciviousness is the promoting or partaking of that which tends to produce lewd emotions—anything tendered to foster sex, sin, and lust. That is why many worldly pleasures have to be avoided by Christians—so that the sin of lasciviousness may not be committed.

WORSHIP OF EVIL

"Idolatry, witchcraft, hatred, variance, emulations, wrath, strife, seditions, heresies" (Gal. 5:20).

Sexual sins are not the only sins of the flesh, however. Paul goes on to list two sins of religion: idolatry—a worship of the creature rather than the Creator; and witchcraft—a secret tampering with, and at times a worship of, the powers of evil. These two terms are also arranged in an ascending horror of evil and indicate that the works of the flesh include offenses against God as well as against ourselves or our neighbors.

IDOLATRY

The word *idolatry* in the Greek is eidoloatreia and means "image-worship" (I Cor. 10:14; Gal. 5:20; Col. 3:5; I Pet. 4:3). However, idolatry also includes anything on which affections are passionately set, even extravagant admiration of the heart (Eph. 5:5; Col. 3:5). Idolatry is the worship of both the image and the god it represents. Herein lies its subtle danger. Originally, no idol was meant to be worshipped by man. The image was provided to localize and visualize and, thus, make it easier to worship the God of which it was a representation.

The basic evil in idolatry is that the creation is worshipped instead of the Creator (Rom. 1:19-23). In this sense, idolatry is no less a problem in our day, even though it is clothed in sophistication. Whenever anything in the world begins to hold the principle place in our hearts, minds, and aims, then that thing has become an idol, for that thing has usurped the place that belongs only to God.

That's the reason that John closed out his first epistle with the passage, *"Little children, keep yourselves from idols. Amen."* (I Jn. 5:21).

This does not refer here to the heathen worship of idol gods, but of the heretical substitutes for the Christian conception of

God, or anything that pulls us away from Christ and the Cross. Such becomes an idol!

WITCHCRAFT

The word *witchcraft* in the Greek is pharmakeia and means "sorcery, practice of dealing with evil spirits; magical incantations with casting spells and charms upon one by means of drugs and potions of various kinds" (Rev. 9:21; 18:23; 21:8; 22:15).

Enchantments were used to inflict evil, pains, hatred, sufferings, and death, or to bring good health, love, and other so-called blessings.

The practice of witchcraft originally was the use of sorcery or magic in religion. The word originally meant the use of drugs, which was later turned to evil ends, i.e., poison. This kind of witchcraft became one means of a broader practice of magic, which, through superstition, was closely tied, as stated, to religion. The Catholic Church has attempted to Christianize witchcraft rather than have it eliminated. Consequently, if the Catholic Church is popular in any particular country, the favored type of witchcraft in that particular country is usually incorporated into so-called Catholic worship.

HATRED

The word *hatred* in the Greek is echthra and means "bitter dislike, abhorrence, malice, an ill-will against anyone, a tendency to hold grudges or be angry at someone."

Open enmity between racial and cultural groups was prevalent in Paul's day, even an approved attitude of life. It was Greeks versus Barbarians, Jews versus Gentiles, etc. It is little wonder that these attitudes often characterized relationships between individuals. All of this is contrary to the Christian ethic and is traced by Paul to its true source. *"Because the carnal mind is enmity against God"* (Rom. 8:7), it naturally results in enmity to men.

VARIANCE

The word *variance* in the Greek is eris and means "dissensions, discord, quarreling, debating, and disputes." The hatred just mentioned by Paul produces variance or strife.

Enmity is an attitude of mind toward other people, and strife is the outcome in actual life of that state of mind. Enmity and strife have a crucial interrelation, which works in both directions. Enmity results in strife, and strife causes enmity. Paul makes it clear that strife, so characteristic of the pagan world (I Cor. 1:29), was diametrically opposite to the unity God intended to exist in the Christian fellowship. Thus, He strongly condemned its appearance in the church. In fact, this was such an important matter that three additional terms are used to deal with the same fundamental issue of divisive elements in the body of Christ.

EMULATIONS

The word *emulations* in the Greek is zealoi and means "envious, jealousies, striving to excel at the expense of another, seeking to surpass and outdo others, an uncured rivalry spirit and religion, business, society, and other fields of endeavor" (Jn. 2:17; Rom. 10:2; II Cor. 7:11; 9:2; Phil. 3:6; Col. 4:13).

However, emulations can, as well, have a good meaning that refers to providing impetus to emulate that which was admired in the accomplishments or possessions of others, as Paul used it in II Corinthians 11:2.

This type of emulation is not intrinsically evil. When one is faced with the success and accomplishments of others, he can be inspired to climb to new heights himself, or he can resent such good fortune in others with a bitter jealousy. So, it can go either way; however, the manner in which Paul uses it in the verse of our study refers to its evil sense—jealousy with an evil connotation.

WRATH

The word *wrath* in the Greek is thumos and means "fierceness, turbulent passions, domestic and civil turmoil, rage, determined and lasting anger" (Lk. 4:28; Acts 19:28; II Cor. 12:20; Eph. 4:31; Col. 3:8; Heb. 11:27; Rev. 12:12; 14:8, 10; 19:15).

One of the most complex works of the flesh is wrath. It actually has a wide range of meaning, which includes human wrath as well as divine wrath. Human wrath is devilish and beastly, which Paul denotes here, while divine wrath is noble, and even though destructive at the outset, always tends toward a constructive conclusion.

Wrath, as it refers to man, can be translated *rage* and, in fact, is a veritable temporary insanity, reflecting a sinful hostility that clearly is a defense mechanism of the flesh. It has been often observed that temper is at times necessary for a well-balanced personality; thus, there is no doubt that anger has both good and bad connotations. However, in the New Testament, healthy temper is always described by another Greek word, *orge*, and never by *thumos*. This type of wrath (thumos) must be banished from the Christian life. The New Testament is quite clear that such displays of temper are sinful manifestations that a man is still in the grip of the sin nature.

STRIFE

The word *strife* in the Greek is *eritheia* and means "contention, disputations, janglings, strife about words, contest for superiority or advantage; strenuous endeavor to equal or pay back in kind wrongs done to one."

Paul uses this word clearly in the sense of personal ambition and rivalry that issues in partisanship, which sets party above the will of God. Selfish personal ambition is deplorable in positions of public trust and responsibility, but it is no less than tragic in the church.

SEDITIONS

The word *seditions* in the Greek is *dichostasia*, which means "parties and factions, disorder, stirring up strife in the church, government, home, or any other place." Actually, the word *seditions* is closely related to *strife* and is best translated as *divisions*.

It is rivalry motivated by self-interest, which can result only in divisions that destroy the unity of the body of Christ.

Paul is not speaking here of differences based on sincere convictions. He is concerned about divisions that are caused by wrong motives that can be traced to sinful flesh. Honest differences are not incompatible with harmonious fellowship because a vital part of freedom and love is respect for the opinions of others even when they conflict with ours. However, it does behoove every believer to examine his heart constantly lest prejudice be mistaken for principle and stubbornness for dedication.

What is true of the individual applies no less to the church. Theological and ecclesiastical differences based on convictions must be distinguished from divisions that are motivated by corporate self-seeking. Too often, when the church would minister to a society torn by class, party, and racial divisions, she can be quite properly challenged—physician, first heal yourself.

HERESIES

The word *heresies* in the Greek is haireseis, and in the sense that Paul is using the word, it means "a truth taken all out of proportion to its accepted meaning."

It is used here with reference to the divisive elements in the church, who form themselves into groups or sects. Such cliques fragment the church, and a fragmented church is not a church at all! Quite naturally, these exclusive groups consider themselves right and all others wrong. Paul condemns such sectarianism as works of the flesh.

To more fully understand it in the Christian sense, it is a doctrine that is true as it relates to its basic foundation, but is taken to extremes all out of proportion to its original intent.

As an example, I personally consider the doctrine of unconditional eternal security as a heresy. While there is definitely security in salvation, to take it to the extreme that one is spiritually secure, irrespective of what one might do, is, in my thinking, heresy. It is the same with the greed message. It is certainly true that God blesses His people, and blesses them abundantly; however, to make the doctrine of prosperity paramount over all else is heresy. The same can be said for predestination. This is a viable, biblical doctrine, but when taken to the extreme, it is heresy. This doctrine states that it is already decided by God who will be saved and who won't, and the person has no say in the matter. That is heresy. It is the same with speaking in tongues. I speak in tongues almost every day of my life and definitely believe, of course, that it is a viable, biblical doctrine; however, as I understand the Scripture, to claim that one must speak in tongues to be saved is heresy.

Another example is the great doctrine of grace, upon which the foundation of Christianity is built. However, to extend grace to the idea that sin does not matter because grace covers it, is heresy. Paul addressed this with two words, *"God forbid!"* (Rom. 6:2)

THE KINGDOM OF GOD

"Envyings, murders, drunkenness, revellings, and such like: of the which I tell you before, as I have also told you in time past,

that they which do such things shall not inherit the kingdom of God" (Gal. 5:21).

The reference to the kingdom of God introduces an entirely new and large subject, and one that is an important and complex idea in the New Testament. Here, however, Paul is doubtlessly thinking of God's kingdom in an eschatological sense (future things). The phrase, *"Shall not inherit,"* carries the thought of finality. The point is that those who keep on living in the flesh give evidence that they are not Abraham's seed and, therefore, will not inherit salvation.

ENVYINGS

The word *envyings* in the Greek is phthonoi and means "ill-will and jealousy at the good portion or blessing of another"— the most base of all degrading and disgraceful passions (Mat. 27:18; Mk. 15:10; Rom. 1:29; Phil. 1:15; I Tim. 6:4; Titus 3:3).

Envyings is a totally evil concept. It has no possibilities for good, except in one case, where the Holy Spirit, who has been caused to take up His permanent abode in us, has a passionate desire to the point of envy (James 4:5).

As it relates to the Holy Spirit, it refers to Him being passionately desirous of controlling the believer so that He can perform His office work of causing the saint to grow in the Christian life. As a consequence, He (the Holy Spirit) is envious of any control that the evil nature may exert over the believer. He is displeased with the evil nature and the success it may have in controlling the saint. He passionately desires that this activity of the evil nature may cease and desist, thereby, bringing about every pressure (short of force) to bring the saint into the proper scriptural mode.

Here is a divine envy entirely apart from sin, manifesting a holy hatred of sin, and caring nothing for its own interest, but only that sin be put out of the believer's life.

However, when it comes to human beings who do not have any capacity for deity, and considering that man is fallen, as well, envy can only be a terrible spirit in one's heart. It is clearly reflected in these works of the flesh and has to do with interhuman relations, which are Paul's concern for the unity and harmony of the Christian fellowship. No man lives or dies unto himself. Sin is a two-edged sword, with honed edges of personal responsibility and social consequences. The greatest evil of anger, enmity, jealousy, envy, and rivalry is what they do to the church. Such personal, fleshly attitudes produce strife, divisions, and cliques.

These facts speak of the impossibility of superficial unity. Such evils cannot be swept under the carpet of compromise or pretense. Men who live by the flesh cannot dwell together in unity.

MURDERS

The word *murders* in the Greek is phonoi and refers to "killing another in cold blood," or even "to spoil or mar the happiness of another." It also speaks of "hatred" (I Jn. 3:15).

When the word *murder* is used, most believers never think of it being used in the sense of the destruction of one's reputation or character through gossip or slander, or maliciously trying to do damage to another. However, it means exactly that, as well as the taking of the life of a human being in cold blood.

The attempt to hurt other people through gossip and slander comes from hatred in the heart and is, therefore, murder. I wonder how many Christians have committed the sin of murder.

DRUNKENNESS

The word *drunkenness* in the Greek is methai and refers to "living intoxicated, a slave to drink, or drinking bouts."

Surprisingly enough, the world of Paul's day recognized drunkenness as shameful and degrading. If pagans looked at this sin in that fashion, one should certainly have to come to the conclusion that alcohol has no place in the life of the Christian, not even in the place of so-called moderation. Even though drunkenness has reference to one we might refer to as an alcoholic, still, all who are in that terrible condition began this journey of destruction with moderate drinking. In fact, this is the sin of any great nation and the greatest cause of sorrow and heartache. Consequently, knowing and understanding the potential of strong drink, the Christian must put thumbs down on any drinking whatsoever, and I mean whatsoever. It must be remembered that every alcoholic started out to drink moderately, but that's not the way that it ended up. As a child of God, whether preacher or otherwise, we must be opposed to alcohol in any shape, form, or fashion, and any amount.

REVELLINGS

The word *revellings* in the Greek is *komoi* and means "lasciviousness and boisterous feastings, with obscene music, and other sinful activities, pleasures, and carousings."

Although *revellings* was used in secular Greek to mean simply a celebration, in the New Testament, it depicts excesses that can best be described as debauchery. Such actions sully the Christian testimony. Consequently, these works of the flesh would place off limits such establishments as nightclubs, movie houses, bars, honkey-tonks, dance halls, etc.

Paul is not laying down a law, for such does not exist in grace; however, he is simply saying that true Christians will not want or desire these things, which stem from the flesh and never from the Spirit of God.

AND SUCH LIKE

This list is not intended by Paul to be all-inclusive and is not intended to be the exhaustive basis of a Christian code of rules. The phrase, *"And such like,"* shows that the writer intended it to be representative in principle of evils that result from living by the flesh.

It is tragic and frightening to realize that without exception, these works of the flesh are perversions of what is in itself potentially good. They come from legitimate desires that are illegitimately satisfied, consequently, portraying Satan's method of operation. Thus, they always remain possible pitfalls even to the man of faith.

Satan is a cunning foe, and sin is deceptive. The Christian, consequently, needs frequently to examine his heart and life in the light of Bible teachings and under the guidance of the Holy Spirit.

WARNINGS IN THE PAST AND THE PRESENT

The phrase, *"Of the which I tell you before, as I have also told you in time past,"* refers to the fact that the apostle was not afraid to name specific sins.

Unfortunately, such preaching presently is considered to be crude, uncouth, and, thus, a wrong way to present a message; however, we must remember this that Paul preached was not something out of his own mind, but rather that which the Holy Spirit demanded that he preach. So, when we read these words, we are not merely reading the thoughts of Paul, but rather the actual thoughts of God. Consequently, they must not be taken lightly.

The believer should understand the following: The Lord does not save in sin, but from sin. The entirety of the idea of regeneration is to make something over after another model. The believer is being fashioned by the Holy Spirit into the image of the heavenly—Christ. As well, considering that we have been purchased by such a great price (the shed blood of Jesus

Christ our Lord and Redeemer), and considering that we belong entirely to Him, it is incumbent upon us as believers to do His will as it regards our lives.

In this capacity, the world is our enemy. Its system is guided and controlled by the god of this world—Satan. As a result, we as believers cannot come to terms with the world. We are in this system, but not of this system. There is a vast difference!

True Christians are different than anyone else in the world. We don't act like the world, think like the world, or function like the world, or at least we are not supposed to do such. If we do, such action constitutes worldliness.

No Christian need offer the excuse of not knowing what is right or what is wrong. The Holy Spirit resides in the heart of every believer, and a part of His office work is to reprove (convict) of sin and to guide into all truth (Jn. 16:8, 13). So, if we engage in wrongdoing, it is because we have overridden the constant warnings of the Holy Spirit, or else, we do not know how to properly look to the Cross. Looking to the Cross will always guarantee the power of the Holy Spirit expended on our behalf, which can always defeat any power of darkness.

HOLINESS AND RIGHTEOUSNESS

The business of the Holy Spirit is to bring about holiness and righteousness in the life of the believer. This is His ultimate goal, 24 hours a day, seven days a week. If the signs of these twin attributes are not obvious within our lives, then we need to understand that something is wrong. We are ignoring His checks and warnings. Irrespective of what modern preachers may say, there are some things a Christian should not do. We have liberty, but it is not a license to sin. It is rather the very opposite—the freedom to live a holy life. The only reason that worldliness is entertained on the part of the believer is because of self-will. If God's will is entertained and sought, worldliness will not be a part of the believer.

No, I am not speaking of legalism or law in any fashion. We are not under law, which means that Christians do not live by rules and regulations; still, out of our love for Christ and desiring to be like Him, the law of love compels us in certain directions. That particular law is not legalism but its very opposite. If it is followed, the grace of God will be obvious within our lives, and the Holy Spirit can do His work of sanctification within us. Such is the happiest, most rewarding, and most fulfilling life in this world.

SANCTIFICATION

The moment the believing sinner comes to Christ, he is made holy and completely sanctified. That's the position that every believer has. It comes instantaneously at conversion (I Cor. 6:11).

There is no such thing as a partial justification or a partial sanctification regarding position. God cannot accept anything less than perfection, and, of course, such perfection only comes with Christ. In other words, when the believer accepts Christ, the perfection of our Lord is instantly given to us. As stated, that is our position.

However, as we soon learn, that's not our condition. So, the Holy Spirit works tirelessly to bring our condition up to our position. He can only do that as we place our faith constantly in Christ and the Cross, and do so on a constant basis. Then the Holy Spirit, who works entirely within the parameters of the finished work of Christ, will work mightily on our behalf. Otherwise, we are functioning in the flesh, which will only tend to bring about more failures. So, sanctification regarding condition is definitely partial, with the Holy Spirit working tirelessly to bring the condition up to our position, which is a lifelong project.

THE KINGDOM OF GOD

The phrase, *"That they which do such things shall not inherit the kingdom of God,"* plainly tells us that a person cannot have the world (sin) and God at the same time.

This solemn warning had been repeatedly enunciated by Paul to other churches also. The believer is not excused from ethical responsibility any more than is the Jew (Romans 2). There was obviously a point of serious misunderstanding here, which, unfortunately, has continued to this day. Instead of ethical indifference, the man in Christ has for the first time the resources to live as God expects him to live. The reason for Paul's vehement objection to the Galatians turning to the law was that it would, in fact, be a returning to the flesh. To do so was to cut oneself off from Christ because that particular course presents a hopeless proposition.

God does not have a double standard, and neither does He view the believer through rose-colored glasses, ignoring his conduct and accepting instead the perfect work of Christ. Now, that is a very important statement, and the reader ought to look at it closely.

CONDUCT

Due to its great significance, let me say it again: There are many who think that their conduct does not matter, but only their so-called faith in Christ; however, the truth is that if we have proper faith in Christ, our conduct will match our faith. As well, it will match Christ, at least as far as a human being can be brought into such a position. Unfortunately, multiple millions who claim Christ are basing their hopes on a fool's hope, thinking they cannot be lost, irrespective of what they do. While the Bible definitely teaches eternal security, it is eternal security on God's terms and not man's. God's terms are those that build holiness and righteousness in the life of the believer. Man's terms, at least when thought of in this fashion, are that he can sin all he wants, and he'll still make heaven his home. As stated, that's a fool's hope! Every man who lives by the flesh, thus, producing its works, is excluded from the kingdom of God.

A FURTHER STATEMENT

Having just made that statement, such doesn't mean that the believer is perfect; the truth is, none are. In fact, the Bible does not teach sinless perfection, but it does teach that sin is not to have dominion over us (Rom. 6:14).

The word *do*, as in *"they which do such things,"* is from the Greek—prasso—and means "to do or to practice." So, the Holy Spirit through Paul is speaking of the habitual practice of such things, which refers to no effort whatsoever to lay such aside. As should be obvious, this indicates the character of the individual. The Word of God bases its estimation of a person's character not upon his infrequent, out-of-the-ordinary actions, but upon his habitual ones, which form a true indication of character. Incidentally, character is what God *knows* you are, while reputation is what people *think* you are.

Paul's statement does not mean that if a Christian falls into sin, he thereby loses his salvation. Not at all! The idea is a habitual continuation in fleshly lusts, even with every plan to continue in that particular lifestyle. When Paul says that he warned the Galatians of this previously, he reveals that his preaching was never what one might call mere evangelism, but that it always contained a strong dose of the standard of morality expected from Christians.

As well, the Lord will forgive as many times as a person comes to Him seeking forgiveness, of course, with an earnest, sincere heart. However, this carries the idea that the person is seeking forgiveness, not that he may continue a particular sin or sins, but that these situations be brought to a halt. The Holy Spirit has told us (even in this very epistle) how to have victory, and that means constant victory over sins of the flesh. It is through the Cross, which ensures the help of the Holy Spirit.

This means that failure is no longer necessary. However, the sad fact is that due to the paucity of preaching the Cross these last few decades, most believers have little knowledge of this great truth, which is actually the bedrock truth of the Word of God.

Let not the reader become discouraged of victory simply because you have been unable to lay aside certain sins, even though you have repeatedly tried. As long as the believer doesn't quit believing, the Lord certainly will not quit His mercy and grace. That doesn't mean that He condones sin, for He never does, but it does mean that as long as there is a spark of hope in the heart of the believer, God will operate on that spark. He will use every effort to bring the person to the place of victory that is intended.

WORKS AND FRUIT

"But the fruit of the Spirit is love, joy, peace, longsuffering, gentleness, goodness, faith" (Gal. 5:22).

Paul continues the contrast between the natural productions of the flesh and Spirit he had begun in verse 19. Here, however, he speaks of the fruit of the Spirit in contrast to the works, of which the flesh is capable, which we have just addressed.

The term *works* already has definite overtones in this letter. It refers to what man can do, which, in the case of the works of the law (Gal. 2:16; 3:2; 5:10), has already been shown to be inadequate. On the other hand, the fruit of the Spirit suggests that which is a natural product of the Spirit, rather than of man, which is made possible by the living relationship between the Christian and the Lord (Jn. 15:1-17; Gal. 2:20).

As we shall see, the singular form—fruit—stresses that these qualities are a unity, like a bunch of grapes, instead of separate pieces of fruit and, also, that they are to be found in all Christians. In this, they differ from the gifts of the Spirit, which are given one by one to different people as the church has need (I Cor. 12).

The nine virtues that are the Spirit's fruit hardly need classification, though they seem to fall into three categories of three each:

1. The primary direction of the first three is godward. They appear to comprise Christian habits of mind in their more general aspect.
2. The second three primarily concern the Christian and his relationship to others—social virtues.
3. The last three concern the Christian as he is to be in himself.

THE FRUIT OF THE SPIRIT

The phrase, *"But the fruit of the Spirit is,"* concerns that which is of the Spirit and not of man. If one is to notice, it says the *"fruit of the Spirit"* and not the "fruit of man." The idea is that the Holy Spirit will produce His own fruit in the life of the saint as the latter trusts Him to do that and cooperates with Him in His work of sanctification. In fact, He alone can do this.

The choice of the word *fruit* instead of *works,* as used by the Holy Spirit, is due probably to the conception of the Christian experience as the product of a new and divine life implanted in the saint of God. In Galatians 5:25, Paul speaks of the fact that the Christian lives in the Spirit, that is, derives his spiritual life from the indwelling Holy Spirit. This spiritual life is the motivating force producing the fruit of the Spirit.

As well, the word *fruit*, as stated, is singular, which serves to show that all of the elements of character spoken of in these verses are a unity, making for a well-rounded and complete Christian life. A work, incidentally, is something that man produces for himself. A fruit is something that is produced by a power that we do not possess. In other words, man cannot make a spiritual fruit, with that being done only by the Holy Spirit.

CULTIVATION

The word *fruit*, as supplied by the Spirit, proclaims to us some of the characteristics of these great and wonderful graces in the life of the believer. Some of these graces are as follows:

- *Cooperation.* In the natural, fruit must have proper soil in order that it properly grow. The idea is that the believer must cooperate with the Holy Spirit in order that the right growing conditions be provided. The Spirit of God will help in this but not against the wishes of the saint.
- *Consecration.* Even though the soil may be good, fruit has to be cultivated. In other words, the weeds around the plant have to be pulled and the soil kept fertile and amply watered. Such speaks of consecration, a proper prayer life, and study of the Word. Fruit takes time to grow, with it not being an instant process. As should be obvious, its growth depends on several things: The condition of the soil, as well as the proper care or

lack of such. It is the same with the believer. Even under the best of circumstances, some time is required; however, as it regards some believers, sad to say, growth is almost non-existent, even though they have been living for the Lord for quite some time. It is this way because of a lack of consecration (cultivation).

• *Cultivation.* According to John 15, a pruning process is required for the fruit to be healthy and abundant. This process is never desired by the Christian but is necessary. As someone has said, "What is hurtful to the flesh is at the same time invigorating to the Spirit."

It must be understood that the fruit does not flow from our own nature. The vices that we have just discussed, or the proper works, are results of the operations of the human heart functioning without the help of the Holy Spirit. However, the virtues that we are now discussing are produced by a foreign influence—the agency and person of the Holy Spirit. Hence, Paul does not trace them to our own hearts, even when renewed. He says that they are to be regarded as the proper result of the Spirit's operations on the soul.

LOVE

The first of the fruits is love. The word *love* in the Greek is agape. It is the love that God is (I Jn. 4:16), produced in the heart of the yielded believer by the Holy Spirit (Rom. 5:5; Gal. 5:22). Its chief ingredient is self-sacrifice for the benefit of the one loved (Jn. 3:16). Its elements are listed in I Corinthians 13.

The apostle's list necessarily begins with love because it is greater than all other virtues (I Cor. 13:13), and is the outer cloak that binds all the fruit together in completeness (Col. 3:14). As we have stated, the fruit is the result totally of the Divine Spirit, yet working through the human spirit. It begins with love, and if it does not begin with love, it simply cannot begin.

Love—agape—is a distinctly Christian term, created out of necessity to depict adequately the gospel of the new creation. Further, agape is used primarily of the love men have, or should have, for one another, which is a reflection of God's love for them. They are to draw their pattern from Him. Someone has said, "Agape is unconquerable benevolence, undefeatable good-will." As such, it is a sharing concern and a caring identification with the needs of others.

This concern is all-embracing, even though recipients are undeserving. It results in the transformation of the loved and the loving. Agape is sometimes misunderstood and confused with what is the accepted concept of love today, but there is a great difference. Rather than being an impulsive sentiment that one falls into, agape is the response of the whole person, involving will, feeling, and intellect. It is not weak and harmfully permissive but strong and disciplining.

WHAT IT DOES

Agape could perhaps be best defined by what it does as well as by what it is. This kind of love must act with outgoing generosity and forgiveness. It fulfills the law (v. 14), providing an atmosphere that characterizes and motivates the entire Christian life (Eph. 5:2). It enables the truth, which often hurts, to be spoken as an appeal and not an offense (Eph. 4:15). It is the cord that unites the body of Christ (Col. 2:2), keeping liberty from becoming license, and building up the people of God (I Cor. 8:1; Eph. 4:16) as they live together in forbearance (Rom. 14:15; Eph. 4:2). It is little wonder that Paul concludes that agape should be the believer's pursuit. He should be satisfied with no lesser prize. Yet, this is not something of his own doing. Understanding the *"more excellent way"* (I Cor. 12:31) is not an easy road.

One might ask, "Who then can be saved?"

How appropriate is the answer: *"With men it is impossible, but not with God: for with God all things are possible"* (Mk. 10:27).

This is perhaps the most significant fact about agape. In Christian usage, it came to represent a divine quality. Not only does God love us, but He loves through us, as well, because God's love has been poured into our hearts through the Holy Spirit, which has been given to us (Rom. 5:5). As such, love, at least the God kind of love, is the fruit of the Spirit.

JOY

The next two fruits of the Spirit have a vital relationship to each other. Joy is the gladness or happiness that radiates from the life of the believer—an outward expression of the inward peace. As such, it is seen and known to others. Actually, this is the atmosphere of the New Testament. A basically unhappy

Christian is a contradiction. The kingdom of God is characterized by joy, righteousness, and peace (Rom. 14:17).

The familiar form of greeting in secular Greek was "rejoice,"
though it probably had no more specific meaning than the
modern "How are you?" It must have had a new significance
to the rejoicing men of faith. Although not the distinctively
Christian greeting, it was occasionally used in the New Testament. The spirit of the word is probably caught in the greeting,
"Joy be with you."

Joy adds luster to all the Christian virtues and illuminates
every experience of life, but nowhere is its glow more brightly
seen than during the time of adversities. One of the first lessons
a new Christian must learn is that joy is not dependent upon
circumstances; instead, trials are to be transformed by joy.

It is not enough to endure or even to overcome trials, for
no triumph is complete without joy (Col. 1:11). Thus, it is no
surprise that joy and affliction are often found together as the
man of faith joyfully suffers for Jesus' sake.

Such Christian joy is not superficial outwardness, but rather
wells up from the deep, inner springs of the Spirit-filled life.
It is a fruit of the Spirit! Joy is the outward manifestation of
inward peace.

PEACE

Peace here is not the peace with God that all believers have
in justification, but the peace of God in our hearts (sanctifying
peace), which can be defined as tranquility of mind based on

the consciousness of a right relationship to God. It means "to bind together," thus, Christ Jesus, through the blood of His Cross, binds together that which was separated by human sin with the sinner who puts his faith in the Lord Jesus and in God.

This peace is not simply the absence of trouble, anxiety, and worry. Rather, it is the serenity that results from living in a right relationship with God, men, and oneself. This peace of which Paul speaks is sanctifying peace.

Let us explain a little further: As stated, all people, when they come to Christ, gain immediately what is referred to as "peace with God." The Scripture says, *"Having abolished in His flesh* (the crucifixion) *the enmity* (ill-will) ... *So making peace"* (Eph. 2:15). Formerly, because of sin on the part of man, there was enmity (ill-will) between God and man. Jesus removed the sin debt by His death at Calvary. Upon man's acceptance of the price paid, this ill-will is removed, and peace with God now comes to the believing sinner.

However, as stated, that is justifying peace, which comes automatically at conversion. Sanctifying peace is something else altogether, and this is what Paul is speaking of here.

This latter peace that Paul is here discussing doesn't come easily or quickly but, ultimately, will come, providing the believer consecrates to the Lord. This means to place his or her faith exclusively in Christ and what Christ did for us at the Cross, and maintain it accordingly, even on a daily basis. This is the ultimate in Christian living. That means that despite the problems and difficulties, such does not and, in fact, cannot destroy this sanctifying peace, providing the believer continues to exhibit faith in the finished work of Christ. This is a fruit of the Spirit.

LONGSUFFERING

Wuest says, "Longsuffering in the Greek is 'makrothumia,' which speaks of the 'steadfastness of the soul under provocation.' It includes the idea of forbearance and patient endurance of wrong under ill-treatment, without anger or the thought of revenge."

Longsuffering is actually patience and is surely a fruit that makes a man like God.

As few other terms are, this one is predicated on God and man, as God would have him be. As God is patient with men, so we ought to be patient with Him, as well as our fellowmen, for circumstances and events are actually in the hands of God.

This vital scriptural virtue must not be confused with a mere classic disposition, being unperturbed by any and all disturbances. Such a mode of life is more of a native personality characteristic than a quality of the Holy Spirit. Longsuffering is actually what it suggests—suffering long without going to pieces. Its primary essence is perseverance (never giving up), and bearing with people and circumstances.

The idea is this: As God has been longsuffering with us, and He certainly has (I Tim. 1:12-16), so are we to be with our fellowmen (Eph. 4:2), never admitting defeat however unreasonable and difficult men may be (I Thess. 5:4). It is this kind of patience that reflects true Christian love (I Cor. 13:4).

Such patient love is not our own achievement. It is the work of God in men's hearts, for it is a fruit of the Spirit.

GENTLENESS

The word *gentleness* in the Greek is schrestotes, which refers to kindness. It is a quality that should pervade and penetrate the whole nature, mellowing in it all that is harsh and austere.

This does not mean that men are to be longsuffering in a moral vacuum. The man of faith is to express gentleness, which, as stated, is actually kindness. In the New Testament, the goodness of God is not an awesome moral quality that would repulse man; it is kindness accompanied by forbearance (Rom. 2:4).

However, when imposed upon, this gentleness can include severity (Rom. 11:22). God's kindness is intended to lead to repentance so that it can be expressed in forgiveness (Rom. 2:4). This kindness in man is best seen in our forgiveness in others as Christ has forgiven us (Eph. 4:32). Here is the greatest goodness to be found in man—to be by nature forgiving. It is the fruit of the Spirit.

GOODNESS

The word *goodness* in the Greek is *agathosune* and refers to that "quality in a man who is ruled by and aims at what is good, namely the quality of moral worth." It is used in Ephesians 5:9, II Thessalonians 1:11, and Romans 15:14.

This fruit is closely akin to gentleness, but of all the fruit listed by Paul, goodness lends itself least to precise definition.

Barkley's conclusion is that it probably means an open-hearted generosity that is undeserved, rather than a begrudging or even niggardly justice meted out solely as it is deserved and earned.

Such generosity certainly gives added meaning to the "kindness that forgives" and, indeed, is a fruit of the Spirit.

FAITH

The word *faith* in the Greek is pistis and refers to "faithfulness and fidelity as produced in the life of the yielded Christian by the Holy Spirit."

Throughout the New Testament, faith relates primarily to the believer's complete dependence upon the work of Christ; however, this fruit of the Spirit is ethical virtues dealing chiefly with interhuman relations. Consequently, its greatest ethical meaning is probably "faithfulness." As such, it depicts loyalty, trustworthiness, and dependability.

As with goodness, man's pattern for faithfulness is no less than God Himself (Rom. 3:3). As God is faithful, so His stewards are expected to be as well (I Cor. 4:2).

Faithfulness is not only to be found in holding true to God under tests and duress but, also, in being loyal to one's fellowmen. Paul's commendations of his faithful co-laborers (I Cor. 3:9; Eph. 6:21) and the faithful saints (Eph. 1:1; Col. 1:2) certainly embrace such dependability in human relations.

Quite properly, faithfulness represents the highest level of responsibility between husband and wife (I Tim. 3:11). No church and no marriage can stand unless they are based on loyalty. Such is more than a human virtue, for it is a fruit of the Spirit.

MEEKNESS

"Meekness, temperance: against such there is no law" (Gal. 5:23).

The word *meekness* in the Greek is *prautes* and refers to the "qualities of mildness, gentleness, and meekness in dealing with others."

This fruit is one of the most difficult to define primarily because it is veritably impossible to translate the word *meekness* by a single English term. "Meek" certainly does not have the modern connotations of spiritless or spineless. Rather, meekness is a blending of strength and gentleness.

It is when we have meekness that we treat all men with perfect courtesy, that we can rebuke without rancor, that we can argue without intolerance, that we can face the truth without resentment, that we can be angry and yet sin not, and that we can be gentle and yet not weak.

Certainly, meekness is to be associated with true humility (Mat. 11:29; Col. 3:12), the opposite of pride and arrogance. This is the greatest type of strength, and it calls forth exultation from God.

Meekness is proclaimed of Moses (Num. 12:3), who magnificently harmonized strength and gentleness in his difficult role. However, the supreme example is found in Him who was greater than Moses, and we speak of the Lord Jesus Christ. Meekness is the very essence of the character of the one able both to cleanse the temple and to forgive an adulterous young woman. It is this yoke that the disciple is invited to bear (Mat. 11:29), for this is supremely the badge of Christlikeness. In fact, Jesus said, *"Take My yoke upon you, and learn of Me; for I am meek and lowly in heart: and ye shall find rest unto your souls"* (Mat. 11:29).

This is the only personal thing that Jesus ever said of Himself. He claimed meekness, and rightly so. It is possessed only as a fruit of the Spirit.

TEMPERANCE

The word *temperance* in the Greek is egkratia, which means "possessing power, strong, having mastery or possession of, contentment, self-control." It is used in I Corinthians 7:9 of the control of sexual desire. In I Corinthians 9:25, it is used of the control of the athlete over his body and its desires during the period in which he is in training for the stadium athletic games.

The word thus refers to the mastery of one's own desires and impulses. The word does not in itself refer to the control of any particular or specific desire or impulse. The context in which it is found will indicate what particular desire or impulse is meant, that is, if a particular one is referred to.

This is the final fruit and could be translated "self-control." Although this depicts the restraint of all the passions and desires of man, it also had specific application to morality. This is understandable in the world of that day, as in ours. Moral purity is a distinctly Christian virtue. Actually, righteousness could be defined as "perfect morality," but it is a perfection defined by God and not man.

It is God's purpose that His children live in the world but remain unblemished by its moral depravity. This is possible as a man walks by the Spirit. This self-control—better yet Spirit-control—reaches into all areas of daily living. Consequently, self-control is a fruit of the Spirit.

———— ⋈ ————

Father, let Thy kingdom come,
Let it come with living power;
Speak at length the final word,
Usher in the triumph hour.

As it came in days of old,
In the deepest hearts of men,
When Thy martyrs died for Thee,
Let it come, oh God, again.

Tyrant thrones and idol shrines,
Let them from their place be hurled:
Enter on Thy better reign,
Wear the crown of this poor world.

Oh, what long sad years have gone,
Since Thy church was taught this prayer;
Oh, what eyes have watched and wept,
For the dawning everywhere.

Break, triumphant day of God!
Break at last our hearts to cheer;
Throbbing souls and holy songs
Wait to hail Thy dawning here.

Empires, temples, scepters, thrones,
May they all for God be won;
And, in every human heart,
Father, let Thy kingdom come.

THE YOKE OF BONDAGE

CHAPTER 7

NO LAW

NO LAW

"MEEKNESS, TEMPERANCE: AGAINST SUCH there is no law." (Gal. 5:23).

ALL LAW FULFILLED

The phrase, *"Against such there is no law,"* presents, as we have stated, an understatement. With an apparent touch of irony, Paul closes his list with this classic understatement that serves to affirm emphatically his contention that all of the law—the law of Moses—is fulfilled in love and its related virtues. In fact, his analysis of love in action dramatically portrays that this is the only way in which God's will for man is fulfilled in its total essence and spirit. It is no less true presently. A life of love under the discipline of the Spirit is the only adequate alternative to legalism and to a self-destructive life without restraints. However, unless the believer's focus is the Cross of Christ, and the Cross of Christ exclusively, there is no way that the fruit of the Spirit can grow and be nurtured. It is all connected to the Cross. This we must not forget.

Paul's primary concern for the unity and harmony of the church finds positive fulfillment here. There will be no strife, division, sects, anger, enmity, jealousy, or envy when men live at peace with one another in kindness, generosity, faithfulness, and meekness. The uniquely Christian virtue of self-control is the answer not only to the triad of moral depravity but, also, to drunkenness and revellings.

It cannot be stated too forcibly that such a life lies beyond the power and strength of man; it is found only in the fruit of the Spirit. Yet, it is available to every man who is truly in Christ. The evils of the world have no power against the man whose heart is totally captured by the Master. He lives in a different world—the world of the Holy Spirit.

THE HOLY SPIRIT

In verses 16-25, we see life in the Spirit, centered in the admonition to *"walk in the Spirit"* (v. 16). It centers up in the following:

- This life requires a great spiritual decision. We must make a choice between a life guided and empowered by the Holy Spirit, which can only be done by the believer placing his or her faith exclusively in Christ and the Cross, or a life guided by our own carnal desires (vs. 16-17, 24-25).
- Life in the Spirit keeps us from the evils of immorality, heresy, and hatred, and it is done as we focus on the Cross (vs. 18-21).

- The Holy Spirit in our lives nurtures the growth of every Christlike attitude (vs. 22-23).

(We wish to express our gratitude to R.E. Howard as it regards his scholarship respecting notes and material on the *"fruit of the Spirit."*)

Inasmuch as Paul used the singular in his description of the fruit of the Spirit in that love is first, which pulls all of the fruit together in one, it has been suggested that the growth of this fruit in the heart and life of a Spirit-filled believer is always identical according to its parts. In other words, whatever degree of love that one has, all the other fruit would be likewise. That means there's no such thing as having an excellent fruit of gentleness and not much of peace. Such would not and, in fact, could not function properly. Whatever degree of love there is, all the other fruit would be accordingly. The Holy Spirit is building all at the same time and not one by one.

WARFARE

"And they who are Christ's have crucified the flesh with the affections and lusts" (Gal. 5:24).

It should be evident to the reader of the epistle of Paul to the Galatians that the warfare between the flesh and the Holy Spirit is both intense and unremitting. The principles of each are fundamentally opposed. It will, therefore, be as Paul has said earlier, that the one who is caught in this warfare cannot do the good he would like to do, at least if he has misplaced faith. How then is victory to be achieved? What must the believer do to triumph? In the final two verses of this chapter, Paul gives two answers. In verse 24, Paul reminds his readers that when they came to Christ, they repented fully of the works of the flesh and, indeed, turned their backs on them forever. At least, this is what happened at conversion, and it definitely is what the convert intended. Now this act they must sustain. Speaking of this radical repentance, Paul uses the vivid image of crucifixion. Thus, he leads us to the Cross.

THE CROSS

This is an image he has used in other places. Actually, it was a favorite with him. However, here he uses it in a slightly different way from the way he used it in Romans 6:6 or Galatians 2:20. For example, in these other instances, the reference is to what has been done for the believer as a result of Christ's death, but in this passage, it is structured a little differently in the Greek. It points rather to what the believer has himself done, and must continue to regard as being done. The proper term to describe this act is *faith*. Thus, the believer in Christ has already repented of his former way of life to the degree of actually having executed the old nature. However, this does not mean that the battle is thereby over forever.

As in an actual crucifixion, life lingers even though the person has been nailed to the Cross. Nevertheless, the believer is to regard the decisive act as having been done. He is not to seek to remove from the Cross what has once been nailed there, so to speak.

THEY WHO BELONG TO CHRIST

The phrase, *"And they who are Christ's,"* refers to those who are true believers. In other words, we belong to Christ by virtue of having placed our faith in Him and what He afforded at Calvary, thereby, accepting Him as Lord and Saviour of our hearts and lives. Such are the men and women of faith who are in Christ Jesus.

The idea is that all who really belong to Christ have crucified this indwelling principle of evil, and in the power of the Holy Spirit, wage incessant warfare against it. Those who are only Christians mentally, or rather only have a mere profession, know nothing of this warfare. But yet, this warfare must be fought in the realm of faith, with the correct object of our faith ever being Christ and the Cross. This is imperative. It is the only route of victory. The problem of the believer is sin, and, in fact, that has always been the problem. There is only one cure, one answer, and one solution; not five, not even two, only one, and that is the Cross of Christ (Rom. 6:3-14; 8:1-11; I Cor. 1:17-18, 23; 2:2; Gal. 6:14; Col. 2:10-15).

This warfare is the battle of faith. Satan will do everything within his power to move our faith from the Cross of Christ to something else. He knows that if he can succeed in doing that, victory is his. So, there is a battle, and there is a fight, but it's always with faith. Do we keep our faith in Christ and the Cross, or do we place it in something else? Always remember that there is no victory outside of the Cross, and there is victory only in the Cross.

THE CRUCIFIXION OF THE FLESH

The phrase, *"Have crucified the flesh with the affections and lusts,"* refers to the crucifixion of the evil nature within the believer. This took place when the believing sinner put his faith in the Lord Jesus as Saviour, and received the actual benefits of identification with Christ in His death on the Cross. However, these benefits were only potential at the time that He was crucified.

The Christian's identification with Christ in His death resulted in the breaking of the power of the sin nature over the life. This victory over sin, which the Lord Jesus procured for us at the Cross, is made actual and operative in our lives as we yield to the Holy Spirit and trust Him for that victory. It is the Holy Spirit's ministry that applies the salvation from the power of the sinful nature, which God the Son procured at the Cross for us. However, this is done only as the believer continues to have faith in what was done at the Cross, ever realizing and understanding that every good thing we have in the Lord has come by and through the Cross. Faith must not be allowed to waver on this point or to stray to other things. It must ever be centered upon the Cross, and, in fact, the longer one lives for the Lord and, thereby, draws closer to the Lord, the more he will understand the veracity and power of the Cross.

A TWOFOLD MINISTRY

The Holy Spirit has a twofold ministry in the saint:

1. Making operative in the life of the Christian the victory over sin that the Lord Jesus obtained for believers at the Cross.

2. Producing His fruit in the Christian's experience.

He is only able to do this in full and rich measure as the saint puts himself under subjection to the Spirit. This is done by understanding who the Spirit is (He is God) and His vital role within our lives to make us Christlike.

This initial act of faith in the Lord Jesus, which resulted in the crucifixion (putting to death) of the affections and lusts of the totally depraved nature, is followed during the life of that Christian by faith continuing to be exhibited in the Cross. This guarantees the help and power of the Holy Spirit on our behalf. Only in this way can sin be conquered, and only in this way is sin conquered.

IDENTIFICATION WITH THE CROSS

Paul makes it clear that those who are truly in Christ have crucified the flesh. This metaphor of crucifixion has vital significance for Paul and is not simply a figure of speech. It depicts the believer's identification by faith with the death of Christ, which actually means a continuous identification. As a direct result brought about by the Holy Spirit, the flesh ceases to be an instrument of sin against which man is helpless. The Cross destroys sin in the flesh (Rom. 8:3). No longer is the flesh an irresistible or compulsive force for evil in man. Thus, Paul can state that the believer is not in the flesh.

It is particularly significant that the crucifixion of the flesh has happened to the man in Christ—it is a past fact of experience. This observation by Paul certainly disproves the theology that teaches that the flesh remains unchanged in the believer.

What a travesty on the gospel when the Cross is made nothing more than sin's competitor and is even doomed to defeat in the competition. Such a mistaken idea results from a failure to give serious consideration to the crucifixion of the flesh. Jesus died not to reconcile men to sin, but to deliver them from sin.

AFFECTIONS AND LUSTS

The specific matter in which the power of the flesh is destroyed is seen in Paul's observation that it was crucified with the affections and lusts. Actually, man's original affection (propensities; tendencies to do evil) and lusts are morally neutral. Their character is determined by what influences them. Thus, the evil of human desires and propensities arises when these natural drives are being satisfied in a fleshly way—contrary to the will of God.

Through the Cross, man is freed from the power of the flesh; he no longer lives by it. This does not mean that his propensities and desires are destroyed. Rather, it means that he no longer finds satisfaction and fulfillment in living contrary to the will of God.

It is in this sense that the flesh with its propensities and desires has been crucified.

THE ACTUAL PRACTICE

In one of the previous paragraphs, we made the statement, "It is particularly significant that the crucifixion has happened to the man in Christ—it is a past fact of experience." That statement proclaims a work done, which is correct; however, in actual fact, there are a myriad of Christians who are having trouble with the flesh, even terrible trouble to the point of it causing them extreme problems. This is true despite the fact that many of them are trying with all of their power and strength to overcome, but yet, failing.

Is there a contradiction here?

It may seem as if there is, but there really isn't.

It is somewhat like a person having a fatal disease and then being given a miracle drug. The disease is then completely cured, with no trace left. But yet, the prescription calls for continued periodic doses of this miracle drug. However, for the sake of conjecture, let's say that either through ignorance or rebellion the periodic doses are not taken. The results are obvious. The patient is going to get sick again, with the problem becoming even more acute the longer it goes, which could result in the patient's death. Maybe that's a poor illustration, but it somewhat portrays what I'm attempting to say. When the believing sinner comes to Christ, he does so by faith in what Christ did at Calvary. He doesn't understand much about it, but he accepts it, and with God, that's enough. However, from his salvation forward, he is to continue to look to the Cross for all victory and everything that comes from the Lord. As we've said repeatedly, he is to know and understand that his faith in the Cross—continued faith in the Cross—is the key to all victory. That is the continued doses of the miracle drug so to speak.

FAITH IN THE CROSS

Faith in the Cross of Christ automatically brings the help of the Holy Spirit because that is the premise on which He works. This is where the problem comes in.

Simply because it's not taught behind most pulpits, many believers are not aware that their continued victory in the Lord is predicated on continued faith in Christ and the Cross. In other words, they are to look to the Cross for victory exactly as they looked to it for salvation initially. They are then to expect the Holy Spirit to do His work, which He always does, and without fail, providing our faith remains in the Cross.

The big problem is that many Christians, not knowing this truth, get their eyes on themselves or their church, with such becoming law, whether they understand it or not. In fact, they don't understand that; nevertheless, that's what happens.

Charles Spurgeon said, "When Christians sin, they go to Christ for forgiveness, and which they certainly should. The Lord always forgives; but then that same Christian looks to the law for victory over their sin, which cannot be."

In that capacity, the Holy Spirit, although very much present in the believer's heart, simply will not work, with the believer then doomed to failure and ultimate wreckage.

It is somewhat like the patient taking the miracle medicine as it regarded his initial salvation, and then resorting to some other type of medicine thereafter, which has no effect on his particular disease. The end result will be that the sickness will return, despite the taking of this type of other medicine.

So, if the believer is not enjoying total and complete victory within his heart and life, which constitutes his everyday walk before God, it is because he has drifted from the Cross, which brought him in. As such, the Holy Spirit is deprived of the privilege of giving His help, for He will only work through the legal parameters of the Cross—the finished work of Christ, the atonement, the one sufficient sacrifice (Rom. 8:2).

LIVING IN THE SPIRIT

"If we live in the Spirit, let us also walk in the Spirit" (Gal. 5:25).

Next, Paul reminds believers that we have been made alive by the Spirit, which refers to our initial salvation experience, which, of course, we have if we are truly believers. He says that if we have been made alive by the Spirit, we are to continue to look to the Holy Spirit—walk in the Spirit, walk by the Spirit—also, as it regards our everyday living. I speak of living victoriously. The Spirit leads; we are to follow. Indeed, we are to get in line with Him and keep in step. In fact, this Greek verb for *walk* is also used of those who walk in the steps of the faith of Abraham by believing as he believed (Rom. 4:12) and by obeying the truth of the gospel (Gal. 6:16).

The phrase, *"If we live in the Spirit,"* could be translated, "in view of the fact that we live in the Spirit" or "seeing that we live in the Spirit." It means that we live with respect to the Holy Spirit.

The Galatians were living with respect to the Spirit in the sense that the new divine life resident in their beings was supplied by the Spirit, as it is with all believers. The indwelling Spirit of God is essential to the new life of the man of faith (Rom. 6:4; 8:9).

THE BELIEVER

The believer is described as being alive by the Spirit. Paul uses *pneuma*, which is the Greek for *Spirit*. It refers to the Holy Spirit in a unique manner, almost fusing the divine and human into one concept, which is actually what it is meant to be. This depicts the Divine Spirit working through the human (the new inner man). To live in the Spirit means that all we have from God is made available by the person, agency, ministry, and office of the Holy Spirit. It means that we are to place our faith in Christ and the Cross, and maintain it in Christ and the Cross, which then gives the Holy Spirit latitude to work. That is living in the Spirit or walking in the Spirit.

It is not necessarily doing spiritual things as some people think. It is all a matter of faith but always with the Cross of Christ as the object of our faith.

This is what makes the born-again experience so absolutely vital and wonderful. At that moment, the Spirit of God, actually the third person of the triune Godhead, comes into the believer to take up abode and there to abide forever (Jn. 14:16). This is why the change in the person's life is immediate and actually continues to change all the days of his life. It's a change toward the heavenly image (Rom. 8:29; I Cor. 15:49). If an instant change is not obvious in the person's life, then that is evidence that he has not really been born again. To be sure, the Spirit of God will begin work immediately, which will be obvious to all, that is, if the person is actually born again.

THE HOLY SPIRIT IS A PERSON

It is of the greatest importance that we believe in the divinity of the Spirit and also His personality. We must learn that the Holy Spirit is not a mere power that we need to get a hold of and use, or something that emanates from the Father, but rather that He is a person who is infinitely wise, holy, just, and gracious, and who seeks to help us as only He can. We must become acquainted with Him as a person and not merely as an influence or power derived from the Father. The Holy Spirit is God exactly as Jesus is God and the Father is God. The Holy Spirit is distinctly called God in Acts 5:3-4.

In fact, the divine attributes, which are faculties of a real person, prove the Holy Spirit to be a real person. He would not have these personal attributes if he were merely an emanation.

ASSOCIATED WITH THE FATHER AND THE SON

For example, how could He be present if there is nothing about Him to make Himself known? How could anyone tell He is present if He is incapable of manifesting His presence? How could He move upon the face of the waters if there is nothing to move as required in Genesis 1:2 and Psalms 104:30?

How could He manifest His power if He is incapable of free and independent choice in doing so, or if He should be a mere influence? Do influences have power of choice and responsibility? How could He search and know the things of God and impart that knowledge to others if He were a mere power of another person?

The Holy Spirit is spoken of as being associated with the Father and the Son and all their work, and as being associated with men on earth as our general overseer, directing us in the work of the Lord as to what to preach, where to preach, and where not to preach (Acts 10:19; 13:2; 15:28; 16:6-7; 20:28; II Cor. 13:14; II Pet. 2:21). In fact, He not only helps preachers but any and all believers in every conceivable way, that is, if we allow Him latitude. He will never force His way, but if our cooperation is given, He will do mighty things. If we are a plumber, He will help us to be a better plumber, etc.

In fact, He is the executive part of the Godhead, carrying out on earth and in redeemed men all that the Godhead has proposed (Gen. 1:2).

THE DOCTRINE OF INTERPENETRATION

The word *in* as Paul uses it in the phrase, *"If we live in the Spirit,"* means "in union with." When used of the Holy Spirit, it does not mean bodily entrance into for the simple reason that the Holy Spirit does not have a physical body. However, it definitely does mean His presence incorporating Himself literally in the believer. The Holy Spirit being God means that

He is everywhere and, as such, can be in as many believers as have come to faith in Christ.

The Bible doctrine of interpenetration means the union of two or more persons together for the same end.

WALK IN THE SPIRIT

The phrase, *"Let us also walk in the Spirit,"* in effect, says, "In view of the fact that you Galatians have a new life principle operating in your beings, then walk in or by the Spirit."

The word *walk* in the Greek is *stoicheo* and means "to walk in a straight line, to conduct oneself rightly." In other words, it refers to how we order our behavior, how we live this life for the Lord, and how we grow in grace and the knowledge of the Lord.

Thus, the exhortation to the Galatians, who have divine life resident in their beings, is that they conduct themselves under the guidance, impulses, and energy of that life. It is life, incidentally, that is supplied by the Spirit of God, which is made possible by the Cross of Christ. In fact, the very first thing that the believer is to learn is that every single thing we receive from God, and I mean everything, all and without exception, is made possible by the Cross of Christ.

Here we have the free will of the Christian who has placed his faith and confidence in that which Jesus did at the Cross, and his responsibility to live the highest type of Christian life, and the grace of God that will make that possible, all supplied by the Holy Spirit.

The responsibility of the saint is to desire to live a Christlike life, to depend upon the Holy Spirit for the power to live that life, and to step out on faith, faith that is in the Cross, and, thereby, to live this life. This fulfilled will bring all the infinite resources of grace to the aid of the saint and put in operation all the activities of the Spirit on our behalf. Since the man of faith (faith in Christ and the Cross) has a new quality of existence, he must actively live by the Spirit. To dramatize this, Paul introduced a vivid metaphor, using the Greek word *stoicheo,* a military term meaning "to march." This figure graphically describes the new dimension of discipline living by the Spirit.

Wuest says, "Paul's central thesis is that the way to gain victory is not simply to deny or reject temptation, for this only leaves a moral vacuum. Instead, the man living by the Spirit walks under discipline. He is so captivated by his new affection that the temptations of the flesh are powerless. The old slavery to sin is escaped by entering a new slavery—a slave of Christ."

THE CROSS

However, all of this—the living by the power of the Holy Spirit and as the song says, "Victory over sin and purity within" —is provided by the Spirit according to the faith of the believer in the Cross of Christ.

Believers are told to *have* faith or *use* their faith.

However, while that admonition is certainly true, it doesn't really tell the believer much, if anything. Have faith in God in what capacity? Have faith in Him according to what? These are generalized terms and can mean almost anything as it pertains to God. Our answers might be these: Have faith in God to deliver me, or have faith in God to see us through.

All of these things are right and valid; however, how does He give us the victory, or how does He see us through?

If that question is posed to us, we think of God being God and using His power to help us.

While that is true, the question should be asked as to the basis on which God uses His power on our behalf. In other words, what causes Him to do what is needed?

We might answer that and say that He does such because we are His children.

That would be right, but none of the things said provide a foundation on which proper faith can be built.

PROPER FAITH IN THE CROSS

While all of the answers given are correct, at least as far as they go, they do not provide the actual answer needed.

As somebody has well said, "They told me *what* to do, but nobody told me *how* to do it."

To live this life in the Spirit—actually *"walk in the Spirit"* as Paul says— means to have the power and ministry of the Holy Spirit working on our behalf at all times. This demands that our faith be in Christ and the Cross. By that, I do not mean just some historical thing that took place a long time ago. I mean that the believer must understand that the Cross was not only the means by which salvation was afforded to the sinner, but also that which affords victory for the child of God in one's everyday living and walk. In fact, I speak of every single thing we receive from God.

Let's say it in another way: The first thing that the believer must understand is that everything, and I mean everything, that we receive from God is made possible by the Lord Jesus Christ and what He did for us at the Cross.

The main thing is that the Cross of Christ gives us victory over sin, victory over Satan in every conceivable way, and all the fullness of this overcoming Christian life.

It was the sacrifice of Christ at Calvary and the offering up of His spotless, pure, perfect, sinless body as a sin offering that made all of this possible. Consequently, the sacrifice of Christ on the Cross is the legal premise from which the Holy Spirit works (Rom. 8:2; I Cor. 1:17-18, 23; 2:2; Col. 2:10-15). Faith in the Cross of Christ is demanded by God at all times, which actually means faith in what Christ there did. We are not speaking of having faith in some wooden gibbet, but rather the price paid by the Lord of Glory. That's why Paul said to the Corinthians, *"For I determined not to know anything among you, save Jesus Christ, and Him crucified"* (I Cor. 2:2).

It is the crucified, risen Christ that provides everything for us and through which the Holy Spirit works.

THE HOLY SPIRIT

What I'm trying to say is this: The power of the Holy Spirit, which enables us to live a godly life, and which is the only way that such can be done, is provided to the believer on the basis of the finished work at Calvary and our constant, everyday faith in that work. We are to understand that what Jesus did is not only to be looked at historically, but its effectiveness is to be brought into our everyday living. This means that we understand that it's the Cross that provides all of this. There must be a conscious, deliberate, settled, confidence and faith that this work by Christ is done, and we are depending on it now for our victory, which opens the door for the Holy Spirit to function as He desires. Then, sin, demons, and devils are of no consequence, for what can Satan do against the Holy Spirit? Nothing!

That which we have attempted to explain is the avenue of proper faith (Rom. 4:3; I Cor. 1:17-18, 21; 2:2). Our faith is to center upon the Cross because that's where the price was paid—sacrifice was made, the sin debt was settled, and the grip of sin was broken.

As I have said previously, much of the faith taught in the last few decades has not been faith in the Cross, but rather faith in ourselves or faith in our faith. It sounds right, but in the manner in which it is mostly done, it is not right.

Faith in the Word is what we're supposed to have, but, as well, we are to understand that the Word of God is in totality centered upon the Cross.

EVERYTHING IN THE BIBLE
POINTS TO THE CROSS

The Word of God—removed from the Cross in any fashion—in effect nullifies its veracity. The Bible is actually one book, and its story is the fall and redemption of man as provided by the Lord Jesus Christ on the Cross of Calvary. How did He provide that redemption? He did it by becoming a man and dying on the Cross, which paid the sin debt and satisfied the claims of heavenly justice.

So, if one is to properly have faith in the Word of God, He must understand that the Word in every respect is wrapped around the Cross. In other words, and let us say it again, the story of the Bible is the story of Jesus Christ and Him crucified. If we don't understand that in this fashion, the Word, in a sense, is nullified.

To be frank, the world—and I speak of those who do not know God—would gladly accept the Bible as a book of witty sayings and proverbs of wisdom if it could eliminate the Cross from its pages. It is the Cross that is an offense to them because it is there that man's sin is fully exposed. Actually, it shows what man was and is, which unredeemed man does not really enjoy seeing or knowing.

Many Christians who claim to have great faith in the Word of God, even calling themselves "Word people," have an improper understanding of that phrase. They try to use it outside of the parameters of the Cross; consequently, the Holy Spirit will have no part in such proceedings. He does not break the law, and the law—the law of the Spirit of life in Christ Jesus—is the provision of Calvary (Rom. 8:2).

Every believer can walk in the Spirit, but only according to the provisions of the Cross, because that is the only way in which the Holy Spirit will work.

VAIN GLORY

"Let us not be desirous of vain glory, provoking one another, envying one another" (Gal. 5:26).

Some have claimed that this verse should begin the next chapter in Galatians; however, that is not the case. Certainly it is the first of a number of specific actions that should characterize those who are being led by the Spirit, but on the other hand, it is also a return to the theme of verse 15 and, therefore, a summation.

The phrase, *"Let us not be desirous of vain glory,"* refers to glorying in things that are of little value.

When one is vainglorious, obviously ambitious to get ahead of others, he tends to provoke or tempt others in some manner. The harmony of the fellowship is thus ruptured.

The word *vainglory* in the Greek is kenodoxos, which means "having a conceit of possessing a rightful claim to honor." It speaks of that state of mind that is contrasted to the state of mind that seeks God's glory only.

There were two classes of Christians in the Galatian churches:
1. One class thought they had attained to freedom in the absolute sense—freedom from any restraint whatsoever. These were in danger of turning liberty into license. This class took pride in their fancied liberty from all restraint.
2. The other class was composed of the more scrupulous brethren—holier than thou.

The former class would be tempted to dare the latter group to do things that the law forbids, insinuating that they were afraid to do them. Thus, the former class would be guilty of vainglory, empty pride, and provoking the latter group to do things that it did not think right.

On the other hand, the latter group would be tempted to regard the spurious liberty of the former class as worldliness and, thus, would think of themselves as more holy.

So, one group was taking grace too far it seemed, while the other group was resorting to law (legalism). Both were wrong, hence, Paul invoking them to walk in love.

PROVOKING ONE ANOTHER

The phrase, *"provoking one another,"* proclaims the sense that they who are desirous of vainglory do provoke one another, which it seems both of these groups were doing. They provoke those whom they regard as inferiors by a haughty demeanor and contemptuous manner toward them. They look upon them often with contempt, pass them by with disdain, and treat them as beneath their notice, and this provokes hard feelings, hatred, and a disposition to take revenge in some way.

Men must regard themselves as equals in their great and vital interests; they must feel that they are fellow heirs of the grace of life; and they must feel that they belong to one great family in order for these consequences here mentioned to be avoided. They must see that in their great interests, they are on the same level, deriving no advantage from birth and blood, and they are on a level as descendants of the same apostate father. They must see themselves as being on a level at the foot of the Cross, at the communion table, and at the bar of God. When they feel this, then the consequences here referred to will be avoided.

ENVY BETWEEN BELIEVERS

The phrase, *"envying one another,"* presents that which should not be named among Christians but, sadly, often is.

Why should a man who is soon to wear a crown incorruptible and undefiled, and that fades not away, envy him who has more of this world's goods? Why should he, though poor here, envy him who can walk over a few acres of his own, or who has accumulated a glittering pile of dust soon to be left forever? He is soon to inherit the treasures of heaven, where moth and rust do not corrupt. Why should he who is soon to wear the robes of salvation, made white in the blood of the Lamb, envy him who is clothed in purple and fine linen? Why should he envy the man who can adorn himself and his family in the most gorgeous attire that art and skill can make? Those things will soon give place to a winding-sheet and succeeded by the simple garb worn by the most humble in the grave.

I think we have made our point.

THE SPIRIT OF ENVY
CHARACTERIZES THE WORLD

The idea is that if one is properly in Christ, there is no room or desire for envy. Being properly in Christ—properly consecrated to Christ—means to look to Christ for everything.

I speak of the past, present, and future—trusting in the Cross for victory. First of all, whatever state we are presently in, if our faith is fully in Christ, then we know that we are in the will of God, and that's all that matters. There is no room for envy in the properly consecrated life. Such does not exist because there is no need for such to exist.

The spirit of envy characterizes the world, not the church, at least it certainly should not characterize the church. All is level at the foot of the Cross. If someone desires to take himself away from that particular place and be removed elsewhere, then he is moving away from the grace of God into the world of envy, strife, malice, jealousy, covetousness, etc. Properly walking in the Spirit will handle such situations.

———⋈———

He leadeth me! Oh, blessed thought,
O words with heavenly comfort fraught;
Whate'er I do, where'er I be,
Still, 'tis God's hand that leadeth me.

Lord, I would clasp Thy hand in mine,
Nor ever murmur, or repine;
Content, whatever lot I see,
Since 'tis my God that leadeth me.

REFERENCES

CHAPTER 1

Kenneth S. Wuest, Wuest'sWord Studies in the Greek New Testament: Galatians 4:31, Grand Rapids, Eerdmans Publishing Company, 1942

Martin Luther, A commentary upon the Epistle of Paul to the Galatians, William Bancks, The British Library, 1791, Pg. 267

Ibid.

Ibid.

Kenneth S. Wuest, Wuest'sWord Studies in the Greek New Testament: Galatians 6:1, Grand Rapids, Eerdmans Publishing Company, 1942

Martin Luther, A commentary upon the Epistle of Paul to the Galatians, William Bancks, The British Library, 1791, Pg. 269

CHAPTER 3

H.D.M. Spence, *The Pulpit Commentary: Galatians, Grand Rapids, Eerdmans Publishing Company, 1978*

Ibid.

CHAPTER 4

Kenneth S. Wuest, Wuest'sWord Studies in the Greek New Testament: Galatians 5:15, Grand Rapids, Eerdmans Publishing Company, 1942

CHAPTER 6

Kenneth S. Wuest, Wuest'sWord Studies in the Greek New Testament: Galatians 5:22, Grand Rapids, Eerdmans Publishing Company, 1942

William Barclay, The Gospel of Matthew: Volume 1: The Daily Study Bible Series, Philadelphia, PA: The Westminster John Knox Press, 1976, Pg. 245

ABOUT EVANGELIST JIMMY SWAGGART

The Rev. Jimmy Swaggart is a Pentecostal evangelist whose anointed preaching and teaching has drawn multitudes to the Cross of Christ since 1955.

As an author, he has written more than 50 books, commentaries, study guides, and The Expositor's Study Bible, which has sold more than 3.6 million copies.

As an award-winning musician and singer, Brother Swaggart has recorded more than 50 gospel albums and sold nearly 17 million recordings worldwide.

For more than six decades, Brother Swaggart has channeled his preaching and music ministry through multiple media venues including print, radio, television and the Internet.

In 2010, Jimmy Swaggart Ministries launched its own cable channel, SonLife Broadcasting Network, which airs 24 hours a day to a potential viewing audience of more than 1 billion people around the globe.

Brother Swaggart also pastors Family Worship Center in Baton Rouge, Louisiana, the church home and headquarters of Jimmy Swaggart Ministries.

Jimmy Swaggart Ministries materials can be found at **www.jsm.org**.

ALSO BY EVANGELIST
JIMMY SWAGGART